THE GREAT WHITE HOPE

THE GREAT WHITE HOPE

a play by

HOWARD SACKLER

The Dial Press, Inc. / New York

for Regina Vasquez Bello

who shortly after sunrise on several mornings in 1915 watched from a window of her father's ranch-house outside Havana and saw the World's Heavyweight Champion, jogging along the road; once or twice they waved to each other, and she spoke of it to me nearly 50 years later.

ACT 1

scene one / *Parchmont, Ohio: Brady's farm*   13
scene two / *San Francisco:·   a small gym*   20
scene three / *Reno: outside the Arena*   33
     CAP'N DAN
scene four / *Chicago: a street*   42
scene five / *Chicago: the District Attorney's office*   52
scene six / *Beau Rivage, Wisconsin: a cabin*   63
     SCIPIO
scene seven / *Chicago: Mrs. Jefferson's house*   73

ACT 2

scene one / *London: a chamber in the Home Office*   89
scene two / *Le Havre: a customs shed*   97
scene three / *Paris: Vel d'Hiver arena*   99
scene four / *New York: Pop Weaver's office*   106
scene five / *Berlin: a sidewalk café*   112
scene six / *Budapest: Cabaret Ragosy*   129
     MRS. BACHMAN
scene seven / *Belgrade: railway station*   135

ACT 3

scene one / *Chicago: a street*   139
scene two / *New York: Pop Weaver's office*   147
     CLARA
scene three / *Juarez: a disused barn*   152
     CAP'N DAN
scene four / *United States: a street*   169
scene five / *Havana: Oriente Racetrack*   171

TIME: the years preceding the First World War

Cast of Characters

FRANK BRADY, *the retired champion*
FRED, *his manager*
CAP'N DAN, *a champion of earlier days*
SMITTY, *a famous sportswriter*
GOLDIE, *Jack's manager*
JACK JEFFERSON
TICK, *his trainer*
ELLIE BACHMAN, *Jack's girl*
CLARA, *Jack's former girlfriend*
BLACKFACE, *an entertainer*
COLONEL COX
DEACON
DONNELLY, *Mrs. Bachman's attorney*
MRS. BACHMAN, *Ellie's mother*
CAMERON, *Chicago District Attorney*
DIXON, *a Federal agent*
SCIPIO, *a street philosopher*
MRS. JEFFERSON, *Jack's mother*
PASTOR
RUDY, *a baseball player*
TREACHER, *Jack's solicitor*
EUBANKS, *his aide*
SIR WILLIAM GRISWOLD, *Home Office Undersecretary*
COATES, *Chairman of British Vigilance Board*
MRS. KIMBALL, *a landlady*
INSPECTOR WAINWRIGHT, *Metropolitan Police*
BRATBY, *Olympic Sporting Club officer*
FARLOW, *London County Council*
KLOSSOWSKI, *a Polish heavyweight*
POP WEAVER, *a promoter*
RAGOSY, *a Hungarian impresario*

NEGRO, *an African student*
PACO, *a Mexican boy*
EL JEFE, *a Mexican politico*
A Young Federal AGENT
THE KID

Reporters, photographers, trainers, handlers, fight fans, gamblers, Nevada Rangers, weigher-in, barker, Temperance marchers, civic leaders, musicians, revelers and mourners, brothers and sisters of the congregation, French crowd, German officers, Hungarian audience, stagehands, Pinkerton men, Cuban boys.

THE GREAT
WHITE HOPE

All lines set in **boldface type** are
addressed to the audience

ACT 1

scene one

BRADY'S farm, in Parchmont, Ohio.

Enter BRADY, *the heavyweight champion;* FRED, *his manager;* CAP'N DAN, *a champion of earlier days;* SMITTY, *a famous sports-writer; several other* PRESSMEN *and* PHOTOGRAPHERS; *a few* TRAINERS. GOLDIE, *Jack Jefferson's manager, in the background.*

BRADY: Get Burke, or Kid Foster. Big Bill Brain! I ain't gonna fight no dinge.

FRED: Now, Frank—

CAP'N DAN: Listen here to me, Franklin—

BRADY: You wouldn't fight one when you had the belt!

CAP'N DAN: Well, let's say none of them came up to it then. It wasn't that I wouldn't, I didn't have to.

FRED: He didn't have to, Frank, but you do.

BRADY: In your hat I do! I know what retired means, and that's what I am. All I have to do is dip the sheep and pay taxes.

CAP'N DAN: Hear that, boys? It's old Farmer Brown!

FRED: **Sure looks retired, don't he! Look at the arms on him.**

PRESSMAN 1 : Three months back on the mill, that's all you need—

SMITTY: How long is it you put away Stankiewiez—

FRED: Not even a year! And if you smoked him in seven—

TRAINER 1: You'll get this one in five—

PRESSMAN 2: Four!

FRED: Two! They got glass jaws, right, Cap'n Dan?

BRADY: I ain't gonna fight no dinge.

CAP'N DAN: Now, Franklin, when you retired with that gold belt last summer, nobody thought it would work out like this. Everybody just thought that Sweeney'd fight Woods, and whoever won that would be the new Number One, right? So when the nigger asked could he fight Woods first we figured, what the hell, it'll keep up the interest—nobody, least of all Woods, thought he would lick him. **And then when he said he wants to try out Sweeney too, why Sweeney never puts the gloves on with a nigger, everybody knew that—besides, he was in Australia.** Nobody thought the nigger would go all that way to him, and even when he did, who would have thought he could needle old Tommy into taking him on?

SMITTY: I was down in Melbourne for the paper, Mr. Brady, and let me tell you, no paper here could print how bad it really was. He'd say, Hit me now, Tommy, and then he'd let him, grinning all the time, and then cuffing him, jabbing him, making smart-ass remarks to the crowd—wouldn't be a man and just knock him out, no, and then, when they stopped it, with Tommy there bleeding, he's still got that big banjo smile on him—Jesus.

PRESSMAN 1: You're the White Hope, Mr. Brady!

BRADY: I'm the what?

PRESSMAN 2: The White Hope! Every paper in the country is calling you that.

FRED: Frank, he lands in San Francisco tomorrow—come on!

BRADY: (*to* CAP'N DAN) Honest, I don't like this any more than you do.

CAP'N DAN: How're you going to like it when he claims the belt's his because you won't fight him. The heavyweight belt, son, yours and mine. He can say it's his.

SMITTY: Just grin and put it on.

CAP'N DAN: How're you going to like it when the whole damn country says Brady let us down, he wouldn't stick a fist out to teach a loudmouth nigger, stayed home and let him be Champion of the World.

SMITTY: Don't do it, Mr. Brady.

BRADY: I'll tell you the truth, Cap'n Dan. I hate to say it, but I feel too old. **I mean it, that's the truth.**

FRED: The doc says different and I do too—

TRAINER 1: **He's thinkin old because he's worried what to do—**

BRADY: Shut up. Cap'n Dan, you know what I mean.

CAP'N DAN: I know you trust me and I say you're up to it— and, Franklin, God Almighty hates a quitter! Listen here, I'll confess something to you, I had this lots of times when I was your age, every time I had a fight or a birthday.

BRADY: How'd you get rid of it?

CAP'N DAN: The one way there is: plenty of heat and nice deep massage. Now, Frank, go inside. Mrs. Brady wants to show you a letter I brought for you. I paid a call in Washington on my way out here, and even though I think it'll make you so big-headed you won't be fit to talk to, you read it, then come out here and we'll see where we stand.

(*Exit* BRADY. GOLDIE *comes forward*)

GOLDIE: Good, so it's fixed?

CAP'N DAN: **Somebody say something?**

GOLDIE: Me. I'm asking, Is it settled please, gentlemen? You tell me Yes I can maybe catch the train.

CAP'N DAN: The man's in a hurry, Fred.

FRED: What about terms?

GOLDIE: What, you expect I'm gonna yell about terms? Look, we're no babies here, you know like I know, my Jackie would fight it for a nickel, tomorrow. But it wouldn't look nice for you to take advantage, so you'll offer me low as you can get away with and I'll say OK.

FRED: Eighty-twenty, Goldie.

GOLDIE: What! **A world's championship?** You can't go twenty-five?

FRED: Eighty-twenty. That's it.

GOLDIE: Well . . . God bless America.

FRED: And Cap'n Dan to be the referee.

GOLDIE: Fred, you're kidding me?

FRED: Him or forget it. You know how it works.

GOLDIE: I don't mean no disrespect, but—

CAP'N DAN: Who'd you have in mind, friend, Booker T. Washington?

GOLDIE: All right, all right. Boy! What else?

FRED: That's all.

GOLDIE: He don't have to fight with his feet tied together?

FRED: I said that's all.

CAP'N DAN: We better set the place.

GOLDIE: Any place, name it, the Coast, Chicago—

CAP'N DAN: No big towns, Fred. You'll have every nigger and his brother jamming in there.

GOLDIE: **For my money they could have it in Iceland!**

SMITTY: How about Tulsa? Denver? Reno?

PHOTOGRAPHER 1: Hey, Reno, that's OK!

PRESSMAN 1: Small.

FRED: No—wait—

TRAINER 2: Reno—

CAP'N DAN: Why not? The good old Rockies—

FRED: Yeah—

CAP'N DAN: A white man's country!

GOLDIE: Sure, but you can find them?

FRED: They'll come from all over, it's on the main line now—

SMITTY: And it's high and dry. Mr. Brady would like that—

TRAINER 2: The drier the better! If that nigger gets a sweat up, one good whiff and Frank'll be finished.

(*Enter* BRADY *carrying the gold belt*)

BRADY: Well, he's not through yet!

CAP'N DAN: There we are—

BRADY: Want some photos, boys?

PHOTOGRAPHER 1: Sure thing, Mr. Brady—

PHOTOGRAPHER 2: With it on, OK?

(PHOTOGRAPHERS *set up cameras.* PRESSMEN *ready notebooks*)

GOLDIE: A deal?

FRED: It's a deal. (FRED *and* GOLDIE *shake hands*)

BRADY: And it's gonna be a pleasure—tell your nigger I said so!

PRESSMAN 1: Pour it on, Mr. Brady—

GOLDIE: **I should miss a train for this?**

BRADY: (*rolling up his sleeves*) You tell Mr. Black Boy to give me that smile when he's inside those ropes—

TRAINER 1: (*to* PRESSMEN) Get it down, get it down—

BRADY: I'll appreciate it, tell him—**my eyes ain't too good these days, you understand, I like something nice and shiny to aim at**—(*Puts on belt*) OK, boys?

PRESSMAN 1: Ah!

PHOTOGRAPHER 2: Stance, please, Mr. Brady—

(BRADY *takes stance;* PHOTOGRAPHERS' *magnesium flares till end of scene*)

FRED: (*leading* GOLDIE OFF) Don't let your boy take this nigger stuff to heart, huh? Explain how it's going to pack em in, that's all.

GOLDIE: He knows how it is. Good luck! (*Exits*)

FRED: (*calling after him*) You're OK, Goldie!

SMITTY: (*to* CAP'N DAN, *looking at* BRADY) Well, there we are!

CAP'N DAN: Oh, he's the man all right. I just don't like the idea of calling it a Hope, I wish you boys hadn't hung that tag on him.

SMITTY: It's sure caught on, though!

CAP'N DAN: That's what bothers me, I guess.

SMITTY: Can I quote you on that?

CAP'N DAN: No, lend me a comb. **I better go stand up with him and get my picture took!**

(*Laughter and* BLACKOUT. *Thudding of a punching-bag, then* LIGHTS UP *on—*)

---

scene two

A small gym, San Francisco.

JACK JEFFERSON *shadow-boxing.* TICK, *his Negro trainer.* ELEANOR BACHMAN, *a white girl, watching.*

TICK: Mix it up, Jack honey, pace him, pace him out, hands up higher now, move, he's jabbin—don't follow them head fakes, you watch his body, there you go, jab! jab! Beauty—fake with the body, not just the head, baby—feint! jab! hook in behind it—send him the right now—no! Whut you at?

JACK: (*continuing his movements*) Givin him a right—

TICK: An where you givin it?

JACK: Chin bone—

TICK: Sucker bone! Boy, you a worry! He groggy now, right, you jabbin his liver till he runnin outa gas an his eyes goin fishy—Why you knock on dat chin! Could be ya done whut!

JACK: Wake him up, wake him up—

TICK: Watch him! He's bobbin, he's comin to you, block it—where you gonna take dat right now?

JACK: Temple—

TICK: How!

JACK: Hook it, hook to de temple—

TICK: Why!

JACK: Softes place on his head—

TICK: Yeah! now you listenin to me, sugar! Hook him again, a beauty, three now—(JACK *stops*) Hey, whut you doin—

JACK: (*to* ELEANOR) Now, honey, you juss know you tired a sittin here, whyn't you go buy yourself a pretty or somethin—

ELLIE: No, let me stay. Unless you mind me here, Jack.

JACK: You mah Lady Luck! I don' mine you nowhere—

TICK: **Oh, long as you lookin at him, he don' mine—**

JACK: But ain't this too much rough-house for ya, honey?

ELLIE: Well—I try not to listen.

TICK: Much obliged!

ELLIE: Oh, Tick, I'm sorry—

JACK: She somethin, ain't she!

TICK: Darlin, you keep sittin there any way you like it, cause he sure workin happy. OK?

ELLIE: OK!

TICK: (*to* JACK) Now, we gonna mooch or we gonna move?

JACK: (*moves*) Hole me dat bag! **Gonna buss it wide open, then we all go out an have a champagne lunch!**

(*Enter* GOLDIE)

GOLDIE: Four soft-boiled eggs, that's what you're gonna have—

(*He does not notice* ELLIE)

JACK: Hey, Goldie!

TICK: How you doin, boss—

GOLDIE: Oy, those stairs—

JACK: Get him a chair, Tick—

GOLDIE: Cover him up first he shouldn't get ice on him.

JACK: Figured you stayin in Reno till tomorrow—

GOLDIE: What, we got it settled there—how do you feel?

TICK: (*puts robe on* JACK) He feel like he look, boss!

GOLDIE: Not eating too quick?

TICK: No, sir, chewin good!

JACK: Ah's chewin till it hurts—

GOLDIE: **Laugh, laugh! This one you have to watch like a hawk-eye!**

JACK: Come on, Goldie, when it gonna be?

GOLDIE: The Fourth of July. Now the newspaper guys—

JACK: (*laughing*) The Fourth of July?

GOLDIE: So, it makes a difference?

JACK: No, it juss tickle mah funny-bone, dassall—

TICK: **Fourth a July an Lawd you knows why!**

GOLDIE: We should worry, listen, will we have a gate there—
fifteen thousand! Jack, you know what they're callin it? Already by them it's the Fight of the Century—twenty years I
never seen such a hoopla! Trains from St. Louis and Chicago,
direct yet, tents they have to put up, it's a regular madhouse,
and wait, from the ring they're gonna telegraph it, Jack,
straight to every Western Union in the country, so like right
away everybody should know, and on that we make somethin
too!

TICK: Lively times, Ah kin hear you comin! Boy, you bout to
win de Fight of de Century!

JACK: Yeah, or else lose an be the nigger of the minute.

GOLDIE: (*noticing* ELLIE) Listen, come here, Jack—

JACK: Whut kina odds goin?

GOLDIE: Brady eight to five. What's the girl doin here?

JACK: Oh, she looking roun. She don't bother us none.

GOLDIE: Lookin around for what?

JACK: You be nice now, Goldie—come on over, Ellie, don't be shy now, hon—she a friend of mine, you know?

GOLDIE: Jackie, you gotta bring a girl here when you train?

JACK: Ah guess so, boss! Ah loves to dance an prance fo de wimmins!

ELLIE: How do you do.

JACK: Goldie, shake hands with Miss Ellie Bachman.

GOLDIE: Pleased to meetcha, Miss Bachman. I apologize I didn't notice you before, such a tumult we got here.

ELLIE: Oh, sure, I understand.

GOLDIE: You're a fan of Jack's, huh?

JACK: Ellie was on the same boat from Australia, she was visitin down there.

GOLDIE: Well, it's great to be home again, I bet. You can't beat Frisco!

ELLIE: Yes, I like it fine. My home is in Tacoma, though.

GOLDIE: Oh . . . it's awful damp up there, ain't it?

JACK: Mm-hmm! You know it!

ELLIE: Yes, I can't say I miss it much. (*Pause*)

TICK: Uncle of mine work up dere in a laundry once, he din like it neither . . .

JACK: Drizzle on you all the time there!

TICK: Right!

GOLDIE: Yeah, well, Miss Bachman, the guys from the papers are comin any minute, you know what I mean, so if maybe you excuse us—

JACK: She stay where she is.

TICK: **Uh-oh.**

GOLDIE: Jackie, look, what's the matter with you!

JACK: She stayin where she is.

GOLDIE: I'm gonna pass out here!

ELLIE: I'll wait in the room, Jack.

GOLDIE: In the room! Jesus Christ!

JACK: You be nice now, hear?

GOLDIE: I knew it! **Last night in my head it's like a voice— Dumbbell, go home quick, somethin's goin on with him!**

JACK: Ain't nobody's business!

GOLDIE: Grow up, for God's sake—

ELLIE: Let me go, it doesn't matter—

GOLDIE: No—please, one second—Tick, go lock the door.

(TICK *does*)

(*To* JACK)

So you don't know the score, huh? Well, I'll tell you the score, right now I'll tell you. And you should listen too, miss, I can see you're a fine serious girl, not a bum, better you should know, so there's no hard feelins here. First, Jack, they hate your guts a little bit—OK! You don't put on gloves everybody should like you. Then they hate your guts some more—still OK! That makes you wanna fight, some kinda pep it give you. And then they hate you so much they're payin through the nose to see a white boy maybe knock you on your can—well, that's more than OK, cash in, after all, it's so nice to be colored you shouldn't have a bonus? But, sonny, when they start in to hate you more than that, you gotta watch out. And that means now—Oh, I got ears, I get told things—guys who want to put dope into your food there, a guy who wants to watch the fight behind a rifle. OK, cops we'll get, dogs, that we can handle. But this on top of it, a white girl, Jack, what, do I have to spell it on the wall for you, you wanna drive them crazy, you don't hear what happens—

JACK: Whut Ah s'pose to do! Stash her in a iddy biddy hole someplace in niggertown an go sneakin over there twelve o'clock at night, carry her roun with me inside a box like a pet bunny-rabbit or somethin—

ELLIE: Jack—

JACK: Or maybe she juss put black on her face, an puff her mouth up, so's nobody notice Ah took nothin from em—

(*Knock at door*)

Let 'em wait! You know Ah done fool roun plenny, Goldie, she know it too, she know it all, but Ah ain't foolin roun now, unnerstand—(*Points to* TICK) **an if he say, "Thass whut you said lass time," Ah bust his nappy head—**

TICK: I ain't sayin nothin!

(*More knocking*)

GOLDIE: Hold on, I'm comin—Jack, I swear, I'll help you, just you shouldn't throw it in their face, Jack, I'm beggin you—

JACK: See? This whut you fell inta, darlin.

ELLIE: Do what he says.

JACK: You go along with him?

ELLIE: Along with you, any way I can.

(*More knocking*)

GOLDIE: Go, sit over there—let em in, for Chrissake—

(TICK *admits* SMITTY *and several other* PRESSMEN)

TICK: Mornin, gents—

JACK: Hiya, fellers—Hey there, Smitty—

(*Handshaking and greeting*)

GOLDIE: Just a few minutes, fellers, OK?

PRESSMAN 1: Well, you're sure looking good, Jack.

JACK: Thanks, boss!

PRESSMAN 2: Guess you know about the Fourth—

PRESSMAN 1: You starting to get jumpy?

JACK: Yeah, Ah scared Brady gonna change his mind!

SMITTY: Still think you can take him, Jack?

JACK: Well, Ah ain't sayin Ah kin take him straight off—an, anyway, dat be kina mean, you know, alla dem people, big holiday fight—how dey gonna feel Ah send em home early?

SMITTY: So your only worry is deciding which round.

JACK: Yeah, an dat take some thinkin, man! If Ah lets it go too long in dere, juss sorta blockin an keepin him offa me, then evvybody say, "Now ain't dat one shif'less nigger, why dey always so lazy?" An if Ah chop him down quick, third or fourth roun, all at once then dey holler, "No, t'ain't fair, dat po' man up dere fightin a gorilla!" **But Ah gonna work it out.**

PRESSMAN 2: What about that yellow streak Brady talks about?

JACK: (*undoing his robe*) Yeah, you wanna see it?

GOLDIE: Don't clown aroun, Jackie—

PRESSMAN 3: Any idea, Jack, why you smile when you're fighting?

JACK: Well, you know. Ah am a happy person. Ah always feel good, huh? An when Ah'm fightin Ah feels double good. So whut Ah wanna put a face on for? An you know, it's a sport, right, like a game, so Ah like whoever Ah'm hittin to see Ah'm still his friend.

PRESSMAN 2: Going to train in Chicago, Mr. Jefferson?

JACK: Yeah, Ah wanna see my little ole momma—

PRESSMAN 1: Fried chicken, Jack?

JACK: Mmm-mmh! Can't wait!

SMITTY: I believe that's Miss Bachman there, isn't it, Jack? You first met on the boat?

ELLIE: No, not exactly—

GOLDIE: Miss Bachman is my secretary, we hired her in Australia, she's from here, but she was over there and we, you know, we hired her and she came over with the boys.

SMITTY: I see—

TICK: Boss, if dey finish Ah wanna rub him down—

PRESSMAN 1: We got plenty for now, Jack—

PRESSMAN 3: Thanks—

JACK: Come again!

PRESSMAN 2: Jack, one more question?

JACK: Yeah, go head.

PRESSMAN 2: You're the first black man in the history of the ring to get a crack at the heavyweight title. Now the white folks, of course, are behind the White Hope, Brady's the redeemer of the race, and so on. But you, Jack Jefferson, are you the Black Hope?

JACK: Well, Ah'm black and Ah'm hopin.

SMITTY: Try and answer him straight, Jack.

JACK: Oh, Ah guess mah cousins mostly want me to win.

SMITTY: You imply that some don't?

JACK: Maybe some a them reckon they gonna pay a little high for that belt, if Ah take it.

SMITTY: Won't you try and change their minds, Jack, get them all behind you?

JACK: Man, Ah ain't runnin for Congress! Ah ain't fightin for no race, ain't redeemin nobody! My momma tole me Mr. Lincoln done that—**ain't that why you shot him?**

(*General laughter.* CLARA, *a Negro woman, bursts in*)

CLARA: My, oh my! It de big black rooster and de little red hen! I got you, you mother!

JACK: What you want here!

CLARA: I show you what I wants—(*Goes for* ELLIE)

ELLIE: Jack!

JACK: Hey!

TICK: (*restrains* CLARA) You crazy, you bitch—?

GOLDIE: A little family quarrel, fellers, see you tomorrow, you know how it is—

(THEY *remain*)

CLARA: You leave my man be, girl, you don' leave him, Ah gonna throw you at him in chunks—

GOLDIE: You got it all wrong, Clara—

CLARA: Yeah? Ah gots it from de chambermaid at the Park Royal Hotel, Ah come all de way from Chicago to got it—

JACK: Now you got it you git you black ass outa here.

CLARA: Don't hit me!

JACK: Whut you tyin on, you evil chinch, you!

GOLDIE: Jack—fellers—

CLARA: Sing it, daddy! Let de gennumuns hear how you smirchin your wife—

GOLDIE: What do you mean?

JACK: She ain't no wife of mine—

CLARA: No which of what? **We's common law and Ah's comin home to poppa!**

JACK: Ah's common nothin! Don' you poppa me, girl, or Ah poppa you so you never forget it! Ah quit on you when you cleared out a De-troit wid Willie de pimp—

GOLDIE: Fellers, please, have a heart—Jack—

CLARA: Ah know you come after me, Ah know you was lookin—

JACK: You lucky Ah too busy to fine you, girl, selling off mah clothes, mah ring, silver brushes—

CLARA: Gimme nother chance, baby, Ah misses you awful—

JACK: Don' come on with me! You juss smelling bread, you comin here now cause you Willie's in jail—

CLARA: How you know where he at!

JACK: Ah from de jungle like you is, baby, Ah hears de drums—
(*To* TICK) take her over to Goldie's, give her a twenty an
carfare back.

TICK: Come on, Clara.

JACK: Ah tellin you once more, go way and stay there.

CLARA: You ain't closin up the book so easy, daddy—(*To* ELLIE)
hear me, Gray Meat? Get it while you can!

TICK: Come on, out—(*Drags her out*)

JACK: (*to* ELLIE) You all right, honey?

GOLDIE: Fellers, now I'm askin you, man to man, please, for
everybody's good, don't write nothin about it, **if it gets out,
God knows what can happen**—I mean, look, we wanna have a
fight, don't we? And besides the girl has a family, what the
hell—(*Pause*)

PRESSMAN 3: OK.

PRESSMAN 1: Don't worry, Goldie.

GOLDIE: Thanks, fellers, thanks—let's all have a drink—(*Hustles*
THEM *out;* JACK *has begun punching the bag*)

ELLIE: Oh, Jack! It gets awful, doesn't it.

JACK: Well . . . seems to get worse and better both at once.

ELLIE: Is there anything I can do?

JACK: Yeah . . . Stick around. An don' never call me daddy.

(BLACKOUT—*sound of fireworks and band music*—LIGHTS UP *on*—)

---

scene three

Outside the arena, Reno.

Across the stage a banner: RENO THE HUB OF THE UNIVERSE. *Many small American flags in evidence. Stage milling with* WHITE MEN *of every sort: at the center a huge crap-game, at the rear a* BLACKFACE *performer entertaining another* GROUP, *at one side a few* MEN *breaking up a fight, at the other a* MAN *supporting a singing* DRUNK, *in the foreground a* BETTOR *with a fistful of money looking for a* TOUT.

ROLLER: Ooh, six, get ready, baby from Baltimore—

PLAYER 1: Shoot em—

TOUT: (*to* BETTOR) Sure, how much you bettin—

PLAYER 2: Boxcars!

PLAYER 1: Let it ride—

BETTOR: Ninety simoleons—

TOUT: Ninety on Brady at eight to five—

BETTOR: Eight—?

ROLLER: In or out—

BETTOR: Up yours eight, mister, they're giving eleven, they're givin thirteen—

ROLLER: Who's in, who's in, who's—

BLACKFACE: (*bursting in on the crap game*) Yassuh, yassuh, yassuh—

PLAYER 1: Hey, look who's here—

BLACKFACE: Move ovah, bredren, ole Doctuh Wishbone gwine ta roll dem cubicles—Uh oh! **Lonesome pockets!** Kin ah come in wiv a chicken laig, boss? (*Flourishes one. Laughter*)

PLAYER 3: Where's the white meat, Wishbone—

BLACKFACE: White meat? Oh, he puttin on de belt now—an dark meat, he shakin in de graby! (*Laughter, jeers.* THEY *all gather round*) **Lawd, Ah sho hopes dey's mo cullud folks den me here—**

ROLLER: Why's that, Wishbone—

BLACKFACE: Ah cain't bury all dat nigger bah mahself! (*Laughter*) Gwine ta read de sermon ovuh him, dassall—

BETTOR: Let's hear it!

BLACKFACE: "Bredren," it start, "kinely pass de plate"—no dat ain't it—(*Laughter*) "Bredren," it start, "come outer dem bushes"—no, tain't dat neether—(*Laughter*) "Bredren"—here de one—"de tex for dis po' darkie am foun in de Book ob"—well it roun bout de place where Paul git off de steamboat.

"Bredren," it say, "bressed am dey dat lays down, **cause if dey ain gittin up dey mought jes's well stays down**"—(*Laughter, cheers,* SOMEONE *throws him a tambourine,* HE *sings*)

Ole Marse Brady whip cullud Jack
Come fum way down Souf,
Hair curl on his haid so tight
He coulden shet his mouf—

(THEY *all join in*)

Coon, coon, coon, ah wish mah culluh'd fade,
Coon, coon, coon, Lawd, make me a brahter shade—

(*Enter* COLONEL COX *with some* NEVADA RANGERS)

COX: All right, all right, stay where you are—

PLAYER 1: What the hell, Colonel—

PLAYER 2: Just having some fun—

COX: Boys, I got orders to confiscate all firearms—(*Protests*) **We'll give em back tonight, after it's over—**

RANGER 1: (*collecting weapons*) Let's go—

RANGER 2: Thank you!

RANGER 1: Say, that's a real old one—

PLAYER 1: (*as band strikes up nearby*) What you fraid of, Colonel, we won't have to shoot him!

BETTOR: They're comin for the weigh-in!

(*Cheering nearby*)

COX: (*to* BLACKFACE) You'd better scram, Mike.

BLACKFACE: Sure thing, Colonel—

(*Runs off; more cheering; a scale is wheeled on*)

PLAYER 1: (*looks offstage*) That's Brady's bus—here he comes—

(MUSIC *changes to "Oh, You Beautiful Doll"*)

ROLLER: Whack that nigger, Frank—

PLAYER 2: You fix him for us—

PLAYER 1: Wipe that smile off him, boy—

(THEY *all cheer as* BRADY, *in a robe and with his hands taped, scowling, enters with* CAP'N DAN, FRED, *and entourage:* HANDLERS, PRESS, *etc.* HE *gets on the scale. Music stops.*)

BRADY: Come on, it's hot as hell here. Let's go.

PRESSMAN 1: What did you have for lunch, Mr. Brady?

(*Laughter*)

BRADY: Nothin! A cuppa tea!

FRED: We'll get a statement in a minute, boys—

CAP'N DAN: Take it easy, Franklin—

WEIGHER-IN: Two hundred and four.

(*Cheers.* HE *steps off the scale, takes out a paper. Silence*)

BRADY: When I put on the gloves now and defend this here belt it's the request of the public, which forced me out of retirement. But I wanta assure them I'm fit to do my best, **and I don't think I'm gonna disappoint nobody.**

(*Applause:* JACK *enters with* GOLDIE *and* TICK: *Silence*)

JACK: **How come they's no music when I comes in?**

CAP'N DAN: How do you do, Mr. Jefferson. As you know, of course, I am your referee.

JACK: Cap'n Dan, it's a honor. Ah'm proud to shake the han whut shook the han of the Prince of Wales.

ROLLER: Don't take that lip from him! (*General "Ssh"*) Come on, boog, I'll get it over with right—(*General hubbub*)

GOLDIE: Colonel—

COX: Quiet down there!

BRADY: Get him on the scale, willya.

JACK: (*stepping on*) Hey, Frank, how you doin? (BRADY *turns away, muttering*) **Look like Frank bout ta walk de plank!**

WEIGHER-IN: One hundred ninety-one.

GOLDIE: Brady?

WEIGHER-IN: Two hundred and four.

TICK: OK, Jack, get down—

JACK: Hey, Frank, you believe that? This man here saying Ah lighter then you!

BRADY: Yeah, very funny.

CAP'N DAN: Just your statement, please.

JACK: Huh, Oh, sure. Ah thank Mr. Brady here for being such a sport, givin me a shot at the belt today. They's been plenty a mean talk roun—(*Jeers*)

COX: Quiet, there—

JACK: But here we is, an Ah glad it come down to a plain ole scuffle. (*A few* HANDCLAPS *at the rear of the crowd, which parts to reveal a* GROUP OF NEGROES *there*) **Mercy me, it's de chillun of Isrel**—Hey, there, homefolks!

BRADY: Come on, let's clear out of here—

FRED: Right—

BRADY: Keep rootin, boys—

CROWD: All behind you, Frank—Kill the coon—Tear him apart, Frank—Find that yellow streak—

(*The* BAND *strikes up* "Hot Time in the Old Town Tonight" *as it follows, cheering after* BRADY *and his entourage,* PRESS-MEN *and* RANGERS *behind them.* GOLDIE *and* TICK *remain.* JACK *approaches the* GROUP OF NEGROES. *Music and cheering gradually recede*)

JACK: Well, how you all today!

DEACON: Gonna be prayin fo you here, Mr. Jefferson.

JACK: Couldn't get no tickets, huh.

TICK: Bess dey don' go in dere, Jack.

JACK: Yeah, maybe so.

DEACON: That don' matter none. We juss come to pray you gonna win for us, son.

JACK: Well, if "us" mean any you wid cash ridin on me, you prayers gonna pay off roun about the fifth.

YOUNG NEGRO: No, Mr. Jefferson. He mean win for us cullud.

JACK: Oh, that what you prayin!

DEACON: May the good Lawd be guidin your hand for us, son!

ALL NEGROES: Amen, amen.

JACK: An you traipse all this way here to pray it, my, my.

YOUNG NEGRO: What the Revren mean to signify—

JACK: I know what he signify. I big but I ain dumb, hear?

YOUNG NEGRO: What you salty wif me for—

DEACON: We folks just want you to preciate—

JACK: (to YOUNG NEGRO) Hey, man. What my winnin gonna do for you!

YOUNG NEGRO: Huh? Oh . . . er . . .

DEACON: Give him self-respeck, that's what!

ALL NEGROES: Amen!

NEGRO 1: Tell it, brother!

act 1 / scene three   **39**

YOUNG NEGRO: Yeah—Ah be proud to be a cullud man to-morrow!

NEGROES: (*general response*) Amen, that's it.

JACK: Uh huh. Well, country boy, if you ain't there already, all the boxin and nigger-prayin in the world ain't gonna get you there—

TICK: Jack, let's go—

DEACON: You look cullud, son, but you ain't thinkin cullud.

JACK: Oh, Ah thinkin cullud, cullud and then cullud, Ah so busy think cullud Ah can't see nothin else sometime, but Ah ain't think cullud-us, like you! An when you come on wid it, you know what Ah see, man? That ole cullud-us? Juss a basketfulla crabs! Crabs in a basket—

DEACON: God send you light, son—

GOLDIE: Time to go, Jack—

JACK: Tell me you prayin here! An speck Ah gonna say Oh, thankya, Revren! You ain't prayin for me! (*"Star Spangled Banner" in the distance*) It ain't, Lawd, don't let that peck break his nose, or, Lawd, let him git outa town and not git shot at—Ah ain nothin in it but a ugly black fiss here! **They don' even push on in to see it workin!**

(COLONEL COX *reenters*)

COX: All set, Jefferson?

JACK: (*to the* NEGROES) Lay your bets, boys, you still got time.

(HE *follows the* COLONEL *out,* GOLDIE *and* TICK *behind him. Lights begin to fade very gradually*)

DEACON: Lawd, when the smoke of the battle clear away here, may this good strong man be standin up in victry. May them who keep shovin all us people down see they can't do it all the time, and take a lesson. And may us have this livin man today to show us the sperrit of Joshua. Give this to us, Lawd, we needs it, and give him light to understand why.

(*The anthem ends and a wolfish cry is heard from the* CROWD *in the stadium*)

NEGRO BOY: Revren—

DEACON: Don' worry, boy. We be all right out here.

(THEY *move back, singing, as the roar increases and the stage darkens*)

NEGROES: (*singing unseen*)
It's so high you can't get over it,
It's so low you can't get under it,
It's so wide you can't get around it,
You must come through by the living gate.

(*The roar reaches a crescendo, suddenly—dies out* . . .

BLACKOUT.

A match lit upstage: CAP'N DAN *in shirt sleeves and braces, lighting a cigar*)

CAP'N DAN: (*speaking over his shoulder*) They better throw away half those pictures they took. They'll be worse than the fight . . . (*Comes forward*) **I really have the feeling it's the biggest calamity to hit this country since the San Francisco earthquake—no, I'm serious. That one at least was only in Frisco. What kind of calamity? Hard to say it, exactly. Oh, I don't think all the darkies'll go crazy. try to take us over, rape and all that. Be some trouble, yes, but it can be managed—**

after all, one of em's a heavyweight champ . . . But that's it, I suppose. He is! I hold his hand up, and suddenly a nigger is Champion of the World! Now you'll say, Oh, that's only your title in sports—no, it's more. Admit it. And more than if one got to be world's best engineer, or smartest politician, or number one opera singer, or world's biggest genius at making things from peanuts. No calamity there. But Heavyweight Champion of the World, well, it feels like the world's got a shadow across it. Everything's—no joke intended—kind of darker, and different, like it's shrinking, it's all huddled down somehow, and you with it, you want to holler What's he doin up there, but you can't because you know . . . that shadow's on you, and you feel that smile . . . Well, so what do we do! Wet our pants, cry in our beer about it? No, sir, I'll tell you what we do, we beat those bushes for another White Hope, and if he's no good we find another White Hope, we'll find them and we'll boost them up till one stays—what the hell is this country, Ethiopia?

(BLACKOUT: *music—"Sweet Georgia Brown."* LIGHTS UP *immediately on—*)

---

scene four

A street, Chicago.

Dressed-up NEGROES, *more arriving, great animation; some carry small American flags;* BARKER *among them with megaphone.* BAND *playing on stage before an enormous baroque doorway, over which is spelled* CAFE DE CHAMPION *in lights;* MAN *on ladder installing the last few bulbs,* ANOTHER *distributing yellow handbills.*

BARKER: (*through megaphone*) **Every Chicago man, woman, and chile, you all invited, tan, pink, black, yellow, and beginner brown, get along down, let's shake the han of the best in the lan in his fine new place here, celebrate the openin, come in you vehicle, come on you foot, don' bring money, just be here—**

(*Auto horns and cheering offstage, then on.* JACK *enters at the wheel of an open white touring-car,* ELLIE *at his side,* TICK *and* GOLDIE *in the rear. A group of* POLICEMEN *entering with them begins pushing back the* CROWD)

JACK: Hey—hey—they all right, Mistah Offisah, leave them cullud come on—

(*Cheers as he dismounts and they mill around him, some with flowers*)

NEGROES:
God bless you, Jack—
Ah name mah baby aftuh you—
Member me, Jack?
Ah wish dey wuz ten dozen—
Reach me that han out—

(*The* CLARINETIST *aims an arpeggio at the backs of the retreating* POLICE: *laughter*)

JACK: (*his arms full of flowers*) Say . . . lookie here, thank you . . . thank you . . . oh my! . . . **Look like Rest in Peace, don't it!** (*Laughter*) Well, Ah am all rested up, an like you kin see Ah bout to make Chicago mah real home sweet home now—(*Cheers*) thass right, permint. Ah don' guess Ah'll be needin to chase aroun fo work awhile—(*Laughter*) an Ah got this joint fix up so's Ah kin visit with mah frens an git rich both at once—(*Laughter, jeers*) But wait till you see IN-side—

NEGRO MAN: You ain't stuck Brady's head up on the wall, man, has you? (*Hoots, laughter*)

JACK: No, but they's a picture of ole Queen Cleopattera whut'll make you set straight—(*Laughter*) an blue mirrs, big chambeliers from Germany—well, Ah ain't gonna spawl it, but say, better tell you, them jahnt silver pots on the floors, now they artistic, but they ain't juss for admirin, you know? (*Laughter. He moves toward the car*) Tick, you gimme a han with these flowuhs, you too, Ellie—(*Silence as she stands to take them, then a spatter of applause, increasing*) Yeah, evvybody say hello to mah fiancey, Ellie Bachman! (*Cheers,* ELLIE *waves, smiling.* TRUMPETER *plays a bit of "Here Comes the Bride"*) Hole on, don' jump the gun, boy—(*Laughter*) An, hey, while you at it, Gragulate mah manager here, mah fren Goldie—(*Cheers.* GOLDIE *waves*) An—

TICK: **See? You black, you juss nacheral come in lass—**(*Laughter.* TICK *springs up, flourishing the gold belt in its plush-lined case*) Brung this lil doodad, folks, to hang up ovuh de bar!

(*Whoops, cheers, drum rolls*)

JACK: OK, stash that away now—What you headin at now is a special brew a mine in there call Rajah's Peg—don' ass whut's in it, jes come inside and git it—(*Cheers*) **Yeah, open house! Les have some lively times!**

(BAND *strikes up "Shine." Cheering continues as* JACK, *cakewalking around the car, ceremoniously collects* ELLIE *and leads her to the doorway, where she formally cuts the ribbon across it; the* NEGROES, *all cakewalking, follow them in, the* BAND *last, continuing to play inside.* GOLDIE *and* TICK *remain*)

TICK: Come on, boss!

GOLDIE: Oh, boy. Oh, boy! You heard what he said? His fiancée? You heard him?

TICK: Yeah, but dat don' signify nothin—

GOLDIE: Nothin! With bills up in seven states against any kinda mixed-around marriages!

TICK: Boss, he only juss now say fiancey so them people don figger she a hooker, thassall—

GOLDIE: **You hear? Take a lesson how to be a gentleman!** It's all, he says. Why can't he give them a chance to boil down, what's he gotta bring her in the open, for what?

TICK: Juss did it today, boss—

GOLDIE: (*gesturing to the car*) Right down Wabash Avenue—

TICK: **No law against dat yet—**

(*Bass drum heard in the distance—continues*)

GOLDIE: What the hell is that?

TICK: I dunno. Muss be some burial society.

(*Enter* SMITTY *and* PRESSMAN 1)

GOLDIE: Go on, take the belt in.

(TICK *goes into the Cafe; cheering, music continuing*)

SMITTY: Lively times, eh, Goldie?

GOLDIE: Yeah. Hiya.

SMITTY: Wouldn't let you in, huh?

GOLDIE: Are you kiddin?

PRESSMAN 1: He came out for some air!

(*They laugh; drum gradually approaching*)

GOLDIE: Look, what's goin on?

SMITTY: They'll be here in a minute, Goldie.

(*Drum very near*)

GOLDIE: They, who's they—? (*Looks in direction of drumming*) What the hell is that—?

SMITTY: You know how they are about places like this. Just their meat, Goldie.

GOLDIE: Oh, Jesus, not here, not down here, I checked it! Not in this part of town!

SMITTY: Anywhere, Goldie. It's one big clean-up—

GOLDIE: **Oh, boy!** Listen, Smitty, get the cops—

SMITTY: Always cops along, take it easy—

GOLDIE: Smitty—we'll have a riot on our hands here—

SMITTY: Really? I never thought of that.

(*They draw back as a trombone is heard, raggedly joining the drum with "Onward, Christian Soldiers," and the* PARADE *appears, escorted by* POLICEMEN. *The* MARCHERS *carry signs reading:*

CIVIC REFORM NOW
WOMEN'S LEAGUE FOR TEMPERANCE
SEEK YE OUT INIQUITY
AURORA BIBLE COMMITTEE
THOR WITH HIS HAMMER, NORWEGIANS AGAINST SALOONS
HEPWORTH UNION
WE HAVE BEEN TOO PATIENT
CHICAGO JOAN OF ARC CLUBS

A lone NEGRO *among them with a sign:*

NO SPIRITS NO VICE

The music within has stopped. Still playing their anthem, the MARCHERS *range themselves before the doorway. The* NEGROES *within have emerged and stand out before them belligerently.* JACK *comes out as the trombone and drum conclude the anthem)*

MARCHER 1:
Woe unto the keepers of the Temples of Baal!
Woe unto the swillers in the sinks of wretchedness!
Woe unto those whose delight is born of evil!

NEGRO 1: **Woe whoevuh break up a party on Division Street!**

(NEGROES *snarl agreement*)

JACK: Easy now, ace, let the man preach it—

MARCHER 2: We aren't here just to preach, Mr. Jefferson.

WOMAN MARCHER: We tell you to shut this establishment down.

act 1 / scene four   47

NEGROES:
    You what?
    Who you squeakin at!
    Get outa here, fishbait!
    Shut me somma this!
    Move—

JACK: Easy, easy—now, mistah, lookie here—

NEGROES:
    Don' argue to em, Jack—
    Shoo em off—

WOMAN MARCHER: Shame! Shame, Mr. Jefferson!

MARCHER 1: **Instead of offering these people an example—**

NEGRO 2: (*squirts a soda syphon at him*) Have one on me, chesty!

POLICEMAN 1: Watch it now, you, they got their permit—

JACK: Hey—

NEGRO 2: Don't shove when you talk, man—

MARCHER 1: Drunkenness, disorder, this is what you offer—

NEGRO 3: Do somethin bout it!

MARCHER 1: We shall not allow—

NEGRO WOMAN 1: Stop beatin on de cullud, hear—

POLICEMAN 2: Look—

NEGRO 3: Hands off—

MARCHER 1: We shall not allow fresh corruption to flourish here—

NEGRO 4: I know that mother, I work for him once—

MARCHER 1: We shall not sit by—

NEGRO 3: We ain't gonna let you—

NEGRO WOMAN 1: Stop beatin on de cullud—

NEGRO 2: Show em—

POLICEMAN 3: I warn you—

NEGRO 1: Git de wimmins inside—

MARCHER 1: Sing, friends—

POLICEMAN 1: Keep back—

NEGRO 1: Juss you make one teeny noise—

(ANOTHER NEGRO *breaks through, begins wrestling with the* DRUMMER: *shouting and struggling at the police line*)

JACK: Hey, hey—

MARCHER 1: Hymn number—

NEGRO 2: You ain't hittin no drum here—

WOMAN MARCHER: Help—

(JACK *stops the* POLICE CAPTAIN *from blowing his whistle, then restraining the* NEGRO, *beats the drum with his hand*)

JACK: Order in de court, boys, order in de court! (*Finally, silence. He picks up the fallen stick and returns it to the* DRUMMER) Now, you wanta play this old drum? You play it. (*To the* MARCHERS) An you all wanta sing? Then you lean back an sing. Maybe us kin come in on it, how bout "Earth Is Not Mah Home, Ah Juss Passin Through"? (*A few* NE-GROES *laugh*) **Thass my favrite.**

MARCHER 2: We don't regard this as a frivolous matter, Mr. Jefferson.

JACK: Nossir, me neither! Cause if we kicks off a rumpus this bran new corruptions a mine here get close up! Now, I pollgize for any gritty remarks was passed, an for not bin too symbafetic on you aims—

MARCHER 1: We are going to witness for the Lord—

JACK: OK—

MARCHER 1: On this doorstep as long—

NEGRO 4: Can't sweet-talk em, Jack!

NEGRO WOMAN 1: Always beatin on the cullud!

JACK: Say, is you brains stuck, or what! These folks been layin down trouble all over, an here, we's gettin included, ain't we? Ain't that good enough? Why, it juss like whut Presden Teddy say, Square Deal for Evvybody!—come on, les treat em right, git some chairs out here, they gonna stay, OK, no use they standin, some old-timie folks long with em here— (NEGROES *begin passing chairs out into the street*) Hurry up, they been walkin plenny too, thass right, Tick, the foldin ones, yeah, thank you, set em down, couple more, here you go—if you all want some samwidges or fruit-punch or somethin, or if, you know, you jus holler out now, OK? We be right inside—

(*The intimidated* MARCHERS *have begun moving off at the appearance of the chairs, and as the* NEGROES *begin to re-enter the Cafe, two* WHITE MEN *and a* WOMAN *enter: They approach* JACK)

DONNELLY: (*the elder of the two*) Are you Mister Jack Jefferson?

(*All movement ceases*)

JACK: Yeah, what about it?

DONNELLY: My name is Donnelly. I'm an attorney, from Tacoma. And this is Mrs. Bachman. (*Pause*)

JACK: How do you do, ma'am. Would you care to step inside?

MRS. BACHMAN: No, I would not care to step inside. Is my daughter in there?

JACK: Yes, ma'am. She is. (DONNELLY *goes in. Silence*) Ah think she be awful glad to see you, Miz Bachman. (*Long silence*) You like to sit down here fo a minute? (*Long silence*) Ellie tole me all bout her people back there . . .

(*Silence.* DONNELLY *comes out*)

DONNELLY: She refuses to leave, Mrs. Bachman. (*Pause*)

MRS. BACHMAN: (*crying out*) Ellie! (*She crumples, weeping,* DONNELLY *supporting her*)

JACK: She all right, ma'am, she all right, Ah bring her out to ya—

MRS. BACHMAN: (*as* DONNELLY *begins drawing her away*) Ellie
. . . my baby . . .

GOLDIE: Look, Mister Donnelly, where could I reach you—

DONNELLY: The Majestic—

GOLDIE: OK—

JACK: Ah see she get there—

DONNELLY: You'd better see a little further than that, sir. I
strongly advise you to send that girl home.

(*The beating of the bass drum resumes, as* HE *and the*
OTHER MAN, *followed by the* PRESS, *help* MRS. BACHMAN
away; the MARCHERS *resume their withdrawal, the* NEGROES
returning to the Cafe. JACK *is last; he turns to* GOLDIE, *now
alone on the street*)

GOLDIE: Well . . . lively times.

(HE *enters the Cafe as the drumming recedes and the* LIGHTS
FADE OUT)

---

scene five

Office of the District Attorney, Chicago.

A meeting in progress. CIVIC LEADERS *facing* CAMERON, *the
District Attorney. They include two* WOMEN *and a distinguished-
looking* NEGRO. *In the background* SMITTY, *a* DETECTIVE, *and the
man with* DONNELLY *in the previous scene:* DIXON.

CAMERON: No, we do not think he's a privileged character!

MAN 1: And still he carries on—

CAMERON: Now wait—(*Consults papers*) Since he opened this Cafe, as he calls it, we have made no fewer than thirteen arrests—

WOMAN 1: He wasn't arrested!

CAMERON: Madam, we have no grounds—

MAN 3: What about that shooting there—

WOMAN 1: You arrested that poor common-law wife of his—

WOMAN 2: He was involved—

CAMERON: Yes, but, madam, SHE shot at HIM! We can't prosecute him for being a target.

MAN 1: Why isn't action taken about the Bachman girl!

CAMERON: She's over the age of consent, Mr. Hewlett—

MAN 2: This—(*To the* NEGRO) Forgive me, Doctor, but I must speak my mind—This connection between them is an outrage to every decent Caucasian in America! Perhaps he thinks his victories entitle him to it, as part of the spoils—

MAN 1: **You know how niggers are—**

MAN 2: Mr. Hewlett!

MAN 1: (*to the* NEGRO) Oh, I'm sorry, sir . . .

NEGRO: We can't pretend that race is not the main issue here.

act 1 / scene five   53

And, as you imply, sir, the deportment of this man does harm to his race. It confirms certain views of it you may already hold: that does us harm. But it also confirms in many Negroes the belief that his life is the desirable life, and that does us even greater harm. **For a Negro today, the opportunity to earn a dollar in a factory should appear to be worth infinitely more than the opportunity of spending that dollar in emulation of Mr. Jack Jefferson.** But this I assert: the majority of Negroes do not approve of this man or of his doings. He personifies all that should be suppressed by law, and I trust that such suppression is forthcoming.

(*General agreement*)

MAN 2: Everyone in favor say aye—

ALL: Aye!

(THEY *rise,* CAMERON *with them*)

CAMERON: Well, I appreciate your coming here to discuss this—

MAN 2: It will not be to your benefit to let it rest here.

CAMERON: I don't intend to, sir. (*Sees* THEM *out*) Good night, good night.

(HE *shuts the door.* SMITTY, DIXON, *and* DETECTIVE *come forward*)

DETECTIVE: Like a drink?

CAMERON: Sure could use one. (*Bottle is produced,* DIXON *abstains*) Smitty?

SMITTY: I'm in training.

CAMERON: You know . . . if a good White Hope showed up and beat him it would take the edge off this.

SMITTY: Forget it, Al. The best we got around now is Fireman Riley.

CAMERON: All right, let's go to work. Bring the girl in. (DETECTIVE *leaves*) You want to question her, Dixon? It was your idea.

DIXON: No, you go ahead, Al. See what you can come up with.

SMITTY: Why don't you revoke the license on his place, that's easy enough.

CAMERON: Sure it's easy! We could close him, we could rap him on disorderly conduct, we could make a dozen misdemeanors stick, but it's all minor stuff. And you heard them. They want his head on a plate. (DETECTIVE *enters with* ELLIE) Good evening, Miss Bachman. Take a seat, please.

ELLIE: Thank you.

(DIXON, SMITTY, *and* DETECTIVE *withdraw into the background*)

CAMERON: You understand, this is an informal inquiry, you've come at our request, but of your own free will?

ELLIE: Yes, I understand.

CAMERON: Good. Now, Miss Bachman—(*Consulting papers*) Yes, I see. You resumed your maiden name after your divorce.

ELLIE: That's right.

CAMERON: And you obtained your divorce from Mr. Martin in Australia.

act 1 / scene five   **55**

ELLIE: Yes.

CAMERON: An odd place to go for a divorce.

ELLIE: I have an aunt there. I wanted to get away.

CAMERON: You hadn't met Mr. Jefferson before your trip.

ELLIE: No, I had not.

CAMERON: You did not travel there to be with Mr. Jefferson.

ELLIE: No, I did not. I met him on the boat.

CAMERON: How did he approach you?

ELLIE: He didn't. I asked the captain to introduce us.

CAMERON: May I ask why.

ELLIE: Yes. I wanted to make his acquaintance.

CAMERON: And once you had, Miss Bachman, what did he propose to you?

ELLIE: That I have dinner at his table.

CAMERON: Which you did for several evenings—

ELLIE: Yes—

CAMERON: Until you began taking your meals in his stateroom.

ELLIE: That is correct.

CAMERON: (*consulting papers*) Where a great deal of wine and champagne was consumed.

ELLIE: You might say that.

CAMERON: Presumably he would keep filling your glass . . . ?

ELLIE: When it was empty, yes.

CAMERON: Ten times per evening? Six?

ELLIE: No, I drank very little—

CAMERON: And how often did he give you medicine or pills—

ELLIE: Never, I wasn't ill—

CAMERON: But the steward reports that you hardly left the stateroom, and that disembarking you appeared quite—

ELLIE: Well, the last day at sea we had—

CAMERON: Weren't you ill in some way? Did you feel strange, or sleepy—

ELLIE: I felt uncomfortable at how people looked at me. I wasn't used to it.

CAMERON: He took you from the boat to the hotel.

ELLIE: Yes.

CAMERON: Did you ask to be taken there?

ELLIE: No, I just went with him.

CAMERON: And what had he promised you?

ELLIE: To spend some of his time with me.

CAMERON: Nothing else?

ELLIE: Nothing that could interest you.

CAMERON: But naturally, since you were staying there with him, he provided you with money.

ELLIE: I have Mr. Martin's settlement and means of my own. He's given me presents, yes—

DIXON: Miss Bachman, Your railway ticket to Chicago, did you buy it yourself? Or was it a sort of present.

ELLIE: I honestly don't remember. Yes, I believe I bought it.

DIXON: Thank you.

CAMERON: You're parrying these questions very well!

ELLIE: I didn't come here to tell lies, Mr. Cameron. I agreed to come, though Jack was against it, because I wanted to head off any notions you have of getting at him through me. I hope I've done that.

CAMERON: (*putting away papers*) Well . . . it seems you have. And frankly I admire you for it. Not many women . . . **yes, one has to.** (*Sits on desk*) You're quite devoted to him, aren't you?

ELLIE: I love him, Mr. Cameron.

CAMERON: He's a splendid man in many ways, really. No one doubts that, you know.

ELLIE: I've never doubted it.

CAMERON: A magnificent fighter. I saw him when he—

ELLIE: That's not all he is. He's generous, he's kind, he's sensitive—why are you smiling?

CAMERON: I'm sorry. It's how you shy away from mentioning the physical attraction. I've embarrassed you, forgive me—

ELLIE: I'm not ashamed of wanting Jack for a lover. I wanted him that way.

CAMERON: Of course you did, and of course he'd want you!

ELLIE: Why, because I'm—

CAMERON: Oh no, I'm not implying—

ELLIE: He could have nearly any girl he wanted, black or—

CAMERON: Yes, I only meant that any man would be proud—

ELLIE: I'm proud that he wanted me! Is that clear!

CAMERON: Certainly—please don't be distressed, we needn't—

ELLIE: Who am I, anyway! I'm no beauty or anything or—

CAMERON: Now, now, you're being unfair to yourself—

ELLIE: Why can't they leave us alone, what's the difference—
(SHE *weeps*)

CAMERON: Oh, there shouldn't be one, ideally . . . and besides, people are so blind about the physical side—a young woman, divorced, disappointed—

ELLIE: Please. If you've finished—

CAMERON: Here, here, now, you mustn't cry, Miss Bachman,

it hasn't turned out all that badly, has it? You have this wonderful man now to love you—why should you cry—

ELLIE: I'll never give him up, I can't—

CAMERON: Of course not, but why be ashamed of it—

ELLIE: I'm not, I swear I'm not—

CAMERON: You seem to be, you know—

ELLIE: I'm not—

CAMERON: Well, if you say so—

ELLIE: I'm crazy for him, yes! I don't care! It's the truth! I didn't know what it was till I slept with him! **I'll say it to anyone, I don't care how it sounds**—

CAMERON: That he makes you happy that way—

ELLIE: Yes—

CAMERON: And you love him, you'd do anything for him—?

ELLIE: Yes—

CAMERON: And not be ashamed—?

ELLIE: No, never—

CAMERON: Even if it—

ELLIE: Yes—

CAMERON: Seemed unnatural or—

ELLIE: Yes—

CAMERON: And when you have, you only—

ELLIE: What—?

CAMERON: Tried to make him happy too, am I right? (SHE *freezes. Pause*) Now, Miss Bachman—

ELLIE: (*with Negro inflection*) You slimy two-bit no-dick mothergrabber. (*Pause.* SHE *rises*) If that's all.

CAMERON: Yes, I believe so—

ELLIE: Good night, then.

CAMERON: Yes. Thank you for coming in. (*Sees her out, shuts the door*)

SMITTY: That's that.

CAMERON: Nothing! Seduction, enticement, coercion, abduction, **not one good berry on the bush!**

DETECTIVE: Too bad, Al. Nearly did get him on five seventy-one, though.

CAMERON: Rah!

SMITTY: **Makes your hair stand up, don't it?**

DETECTIVE: Sure does. She's like a kid with a piece of chocolate cake.

CAMERON: All right! It's a rotten job . . . ! (*To* DIXON) So, what do you think? Any hope of a Federal slap here?

DIXON: I'm not sure yet, Al. I'll need to have a word with the fine-print boys. And I'd like to speak to Donnelly—OK?

(DETECTIVE *leaves*)

CAMERON: But what's there to move on? The railway ticket?

DIXON: Well, maybe not that, exactly. I doubt if we could prove he actually bought it—

CAMERON: And say you could—so?

DIXON: It's occurred to me, Al—seeing how we've just drawn a blank everywhere else—that we might just nail him with the Mann Act.

CAMERON: What? But that's for commercial ass, not this. She's not a pro!

DIXON: Yes, I know that, Al. But there is a law against "transporting a person across a state line for immoral purposes."

CAMERON: No riders, nothing about "intent to gain" or "against volition"?

DIXON: I don't believe so. (DONNELLY *enters with* DETECTIVE) Oh, good evening, Mr. Donnelly. We've spoken to your young lady—

DONNELLY: Yes? And—?

DIXON: You'll remember that our office agreed, at the outset, not to involve her in any proceedings unless it was absolutely necessary. Unfortunately, now, Mr. Donnelly, it may be, and we shall probably require certain evidence. We thought you should know this beforehand, so that you may return to Tacoma and prepare your principal.

DONNELLY: I understand, sir.

DIXON: Good. Thank you.

CAMERON: **I'll have that bastard watched day and night!**

DIXON: Don't bother, Al. We've done it right along.

(BLACKOUT. *Sound of crickets chirping.* LIGHTS UP *on—*)

scene six

A cabin, Beau Rivage, Wisconsin.

ELLIE *sitting up in bed, a sheet around her.* JACK, *wrapped in a towel, beside her. Kerosene lamp.*

JACK: Shucks, honey, it ain't cold, this the finest time for swimmin—

ELLIE: We have come to a parting of the ways.

JACK: Aw . . . big silvery moon, pine trees—

ELLIE: Snapping turtles, moccasins—

JACK: **Lawd, whut to do when romance done gone!**

ELLIE: Oh, Jack, I couldn't make it to the door.

JACK: That right? Sposin Ah carry you down there then an sorta—

ELLIE: No—

JACK: Ease you in—

ELLIE: No! No fair—Jack!—don't tickle me—

JACK: Mmm, she a reglah—

ELLIE: Please—no!—Ow!—Jack, that hurts—

JACK: Hey, baby, Ah didn—

ELLIE: I know, this damn sunburn.

JACK: Aw, Ah'm sorry—here, lemme pat somethin on it—
(*Takes up a champagne bottle, applies some to her back*)
Yeah . . .

ELLIE: Oh, thanks . . . ooh . . . oh, yes, it's—Jack?

JACK: Don' that feel good now?

ELLIE: What are—?

JACK: Cool—?

ELLIE: Not champagne, Jack!

JACK: Well, thass alright, baby, you worth the bess.

ELLIE: All over me . . .

JACK: Get some lake on you, huh?

ELLIE: No, I—(*Peering at him*) Jack, turn around a little . . .
more, this way . . . Are you feeling all right?

JACK: Ah ain't feelin no diffrunt.

ELLIE: Are you sure?

JACK: Yeah!

ELLIE: You ate all those clams, maybe you—(*Feels his head*)

JACK: Whut you doin that for, ain't got no fever—

ELLIE: Well, you look—a little peculiar, Jack.

JACK: Oh . . . ? Kinda ashy, you mean?

ELLIE: Yes, a sort of funny—

JACK: Honey, that ain't sick, that how Ah gets a sunburn. (ELLIE *tries not to laugh*) Now what you laughin at—

ELLIE: I thought—I mean—oh!—oh, Jack—

JACK: Huh?

ELLIE: I can't help it, I'm sorry—how you—oh—

JACK: Yeah—come on, that ain't nice—(HE *starts to laugh*) You thought what, honey?

ELLIE: I—I thought it just—bounces off, that's all—(BOTH *laugh uproariously*)

JACK: Bounces off—

ELLIE: Yes—

JACK: Well, Miss Medium Rare, meet Mr. Well Done! (*Gales of laughter*) **Yeah . . . lotta folks better off in de shade.**

ELLIE: Oh . . . do we have to leave tomorrow?

JACK: Shouldn't leave the place alone too long, honey.

ELLIE: I know. All right.

JACK: Case there's any fussin or—

ELLIE: Ssh, I know.

JACK: My, you do smell good though.

ELLIE: Yes?

JACK: Mm-hmm.

ELLIE: You're not tired of being alone with me, are you?

JACK: Hey. You kiddin?

ELLIE: Or tired of me asking questions like that?

JACK: Oh . . . Ah'm gettin tired of plenny . . . but, no, you ain't in there at all.

ELLIE: It's lovely to hear you say that . . .

JACK: Yeah? . . . Well, OK then . . . (*Props himself up*) How you doin for pillers?

ELLIE: Fine, darling . . . (JACK *hums a little*) Have a swim if you want to.

JACK: No, Ah'm cozy here . . . I cozy, an you rosy . . .

(ELLIE *chuckles.* JACK *turns the lamp down very low, kisses her, draws away. Sings softly*)

Good morning, blues
Blues, how do you do,
Blues say, Ah all right,
Brother, how are you.
Woke up dis mornin,
Blues all round mah head,
Look down to mah breakfas,
Blues all in mah bread . . .
For how long, how long,
Ah sayin, how long . . .

ELLIE: Lying in the sun I was, you know daydreaming . . . how maybe I'd stay there . . . and it would keep on burning me . . . day after day . . . oh, right through September . . . And I'd get darker and darker . . . I really get dark, you know . . . and then I'd dye my hair . . . and I'd change my name . . . and I'd come to you in Chicago . . . like somebody new . . . a colored woman, or a Creole maybe . . . and nobody but you would ever guess . . .

JACK: Won't work, honey.

ELLIE: Hm?

JACK: Evvybody know Ah gone off cullud women.

ELLIE: Oh, Jack, don't tease . . .

JACK: **Ah has, too, 'cep for mah momma.**

ELLIE: Maybe if I . . .

JACK: Ssh.

ELLIE: What will we do . . .

JACK: Ssh . . . try an sleep, honey . . . (*Turns the lamp down a little further*) Creepin up on me a little too—(*Darkness. Sings*) For how long, how long, Ah sayin . . . Always callin you honey, ain't Ah.

ELLIE: Mm.

JACK: Don' remember Ah call no woman by that. Call em by their name . . . or juss "baby," you know . . . Don' ever call you by you name, Ah guess . . .

ELLIE: Hardly ever . . .

JACK: Muss be some kinda ju-ju Ah fraid of in it . . . like if Ah says it you maybe disappear on me . . .

ELLIE: Oh . . . I don't care about my name . . .

JACK: Honey . . . hit just right . . .

ELLIE: Yes . . .

JACK: Honey fum the bees . . . (SHE *sighs*) Ever look at it real, real good a while . . . ?

ELLIE: Can't remember . . .

JACK: Nothin like that stuff . . . Used to sit . . . Oh, long time ago, in Texas . . . we-all ud have a lil honey-treat sometime . . . whole yellah mugful . . . used to set there with it till evvybody come in . . . foolin with it, you know . . . liff up a spoonful . . . tip it a lil bit . . . watch it start to curve up . . . start in to sli-i-i-de ovuh . . . oh, takin its time . . . slow . . . slow . . . honey underneath waitin . . . honey hanging ovuh it . . . hundred years up there . . . then down . . . stringing down . . . down . . . tiny lil dent where it touch . . . an then . . . (*Suddenly embracing her*) Oh, mah sweet, sweet baby, Ah want to have it all—

ELLIE: Yes—

(*Sound of a door splintered open.* SIX MEN—*two with lanterns —burst in. Confusion of light and bodies*)

MAN 1: On your feet, Jefferson—

ELLIE: Jack—

MAN 2: Get the window, Charlie—

MAN 3: Hey—

MAN 1: Look out—

MAN 4: Oh!

MAN 5: Grab him—

MAN 4: He's—chokin me—

MAN 1: Here, you—

(*Thud.* ELLIE *screams*)

MAN 1: Let go or I'll put a hole in you—

MAN 2: Where is he—

MAN 1: I said—

(*Thud*)

ELLIE: Stop it—

MAN 4: Jesus—

MAN 6: Light that goddamn lamp—

ELLIE: Please—

MAN 5: Sit there, lady—

MAN 1: We're the law.

(*Kerosene lamp on.* ELLIE *huddled at the head of the bed,* JACK *crouching in a corner, grasping a chunk of firewood, the injured* MAN *nursing his neck, the* OTHERS *facing* JACK, *immobile*—DIXON *is among them,* ALL *breathing heavily.* DIXON *moves forward*)

DIXON: I'm a federal marshal, Jefferson. (*Shows his badge*) Put that down, please. (*Pause*) Come on. We don't want to make this any worse. (*Pause.* JACK *drops wood*) At ten A.M. this morning you drove Miss Eleanor Bachman across the Illinois-Wisconsin state line. Having done so, you proceeded to have relations with her. Under the Mann Act this makes you liable and I'm therefore placing you under arrest.

ELLIE: No . . . no . . .

DIXON: Get dressed, please, Miss Bachman. We'll take you into town.

ELLIE: Jack—

JACK: Don't worry—get dress—(*Handing her her clothes*)

MAN 2: Here.

DIXON: Hold a blanket up or something.

ELLIE: Jack . . .

JACK: Don't you fret now . . . (MAN 2 *and* MAN 3 *screen her with a blanket. To* DIXON) Thanks, mistah.

DIXON: Sure.

JACK: (*pulling on a sweater*) How much this carry?

DIXON: One to three.

JACK: She clear?

DIXON: Just you.

JACK: Yeah. Thanks.

MAN 1: (*showing handcuffs*) We need these, Jim?

DIXON: No. Find him his pants and let's get out of here.

(BLACKOUT. *Soft, woeful singing in the darkness, which continues through the following. A bizarre-looking colored man comes forward:* SCIPIO. HE *wears a shabby purple cloak fastened with a gold clasp over a shabby dark suit, a bowler hat with a long plume hanging from it, fawn shoes, and several large totemic-looking rings. His manner is feverish*)

SCIPIO: (*speaking over his shoulder into the darkness*) Start it up, thassit, brothers, singing and moanin! White man juss drag him another away here so all you black flies, you light down together an hum pretty please to white man's Jesus—Yes, Lawd! (*Spits*) Waste a mah times . . . **An Ah don' care to talk to you neither! But Ah sees two-three out there de same blood is me, so Ah says good-evenin to em, then Ah askin em this: How much white you up to? How much you done took on? How much white you pinin for? How white you wanna be? Oh, mebbe you done school youself away fum White Jesus—**

but how long you evah turn you heart away frum WHITE! How you lookin, how you movin, how you wishin an figgering— how white you wanna be, that whut Ah askin! How white you gaunta get—you tell me! You watchin that boy? Nothin white-y bout him, huh? But whut he hustle after? White man's sportin prize! Whut he gotta itch for? White man's poontang! Whut his rich livin like? White man's nigger! Thinks he walkin and talkin like a natchul man, don' know how he's swimmin half-drownded in the whitewash, like they is, like you is, nevah done diffrunt, gulpin it in evvy day, pickled in it, right at home dere—tell me that ain't how we living! Tell me how it better you chokin on dat whitewash then wearin a iron colluh roun you neck! Oh, yeah, you sayin, but whut kin we do, Whut kin us or dat boy or dem gospellers do, we passin our days in de white man's world—well, make you own, brothers! Don' try an join em an don' try an beat em, leave em all at once, all together, pack up! Colleck you wages, grab whutevah here gonna come in handy an sluff off de ress! Time to get it goin! Time again to make us a big new wise proud dark man's world—again! Ah says again! Ah tellin what we had once! Nevah mine that singing—learn, brothers, learn! Ee-gyp!! Tambuctoo!! Ethiopya!! Red 'n goldin cities older den Jeruslem, temples an prayin to sperrits whut stick wid us, black men carvin ivory, workin up laws, chartin em maps for de moon an de sun, refine' cultured cullud people hansome as statues dere when Europe an all was juss woods fulla hairy cannibals—dat laughin don' harm us none! Five hundrid million of us not all together, not matchin up to em, dat what harmin us! Dream bout it, brothers—Five hundrid million on dey own part of de earth, an not a one dere evah askin another, How much white you up to, how white you wanna be . . .

(*Glaring,* HE *makes his exit as* LIGHTS COME UP *on—*)

scene seven

Mrs. Jefferson's house, Chicago.

Surrounding MRS. JEFFERSON *in her armchair are the* PASTOR *and seven or eight* BROTHERS *and* SISTERS, *who continue singing softly, as the* PASTOR *speaks. At one side is* CLARA, *now dressed rather plainly.* MRS. JEFFERSON *wears a nightdress, with a shawl over her shoulders and another covering her legs.*

PASTOR: Lawd, we prayin longside this sick unhappy mother here, she lookin to You, Lawd, she know her boy been sinful, an she sorry about that, but she do love him, Lawd, you give him another chance she nevah ask you for anythin! She living by You Book all her days, Lawd, you seen it! We prayin you touch them judges' eyes with mercy. Let em chastise him today, Lawd, let em fine him so steep he leff withouta dime, let em scare him so hard he nevah forgit it, but, Lawd, don' let em lock this woman's boy away.

(End singing)

BROTHERS: Amen.

MRS. JEFFERSON: An if they does, Oh please, Lawd, let it juss be for a little.

BROTHERS: Amen.

PASTOR: We callin with you, sister.

MRS. JEFFERSON: Ah thank ya, Pastor. Wish Ah could offuh ya some lil hospitality but honess—

PASTOR: Don' fret now, sister.

MRS. JEFFERSON: Ah mean, Ah kin hardly—

SISTER 1: Nevah you mine, Tiny.

CLARA: Ah'll put on a potta fresh cawfee—(*Starts to go*)

MRS. JEFFERSON: See if Tick or somebody comin down the street firss.

(CLARA *goes to the window*)

SISTER 2: Early yet, sister.

CLARA: Juss a buncha fellers there gawnta play baseball.

MRS. JEFFERSON: (*sighs*) Awright, Clara. Thankya.

PASTOR: (*as* CLARA *goes to kitchen*) Got a guardjin angel with that gal in you house.

BROTHER 1: Who deserve one better!

(BROTHERS *approve*)

MRS. JEFFERSON: Should've brung word by this. Caint've took this long.

PASTOR: We in de Lawd's hans, sister.

BROTHERS: Amen.

SISTER 1: You sit easy . . .

MRS. JEFFERSON: Fum when he was chile Ah knowed this day comin. Looka that, Momma, why cain't Ah, Momma, lemme lone, Momma. Nevah stop. Fidgety feet an, oh, them great big eyes, roamin an reachin, all ovuh. Tried to learn him like you gotta learn a cullud boy, Dass'nt, dass'nt, dass'nt, that ain't for you! Roll right off him. Tried to learn it to him meaner—**Mo chile you got, the meaner you go to if you lovin you chile. That plain cullud sense.** Hit him with my han, he say, So what. Hit him with my shoe, he look up an smile. Took a razor-strop to him, that make him squint but then he do a funny dance an ask me fo a nickel. Ah prayed to de Lawd put mo strenf in my arm, the worse Ah was whippin the bigger he growed, leven years old an still woulden hear nothin. Hit him with a stick till Ah coulden hit no mo, he pull it away fum me, an bust it in two, and then he run off—

PASTOR: Sister—

MRS. JEFFERSON: Lawd fogive me treatin him so mean! Lawd fogive me not beatin on him young enough or hurtin him bad enough to learn him after, cause Ah seen this day comin—

(*Knock downstairs*)

SISTER 1: Ah let em in, Tiny. (*Goes*)

PASTOR: We hopin with you, sister. Hole onter my han now.

MRS. JEFFERSON: No, thass awright.

SISTER 1: (*offstage*) But you all muss ain't got de right house—

RUDY: (*offstage*) Two thirty-one?

TEAMMATE: (*offstage*) Miz Jeffson's house, ain't it?

SISTER 1: (*closer*) Yeah, but—hang on, whole lotta you cain't fit here—

RUDY: OK, set on de stairway, de ress of you—(SISTER 1 *backs into the room, followed by three large* YOUNG NEGROES *wearing blue satin jackets and matching baseball caps.* THEY *carry valises from which bats and other gear protrude. Their leader, and the largest,* RUDY, *takes off his cap and the* OTHERS *follow suit.* CLARA *re-enters from the kitchen*) Aftuhnoon, evvybody.

MRS. JEFFERSON: You all comin fum de courthouse?

RUDY: No ma'am. Us juss get a message—uh—askin we pay a call here. We de Blue Jays.

MRS. JEFFERSON: You de which?

RUDY: De-troit Blue Jays. You know, de cullud baseball club? **Pulvrise de Afro Giants here Sadday?**

BROTHER 2: Oh, yeah, my nephew tend dat game.

RUDY: My name Rudy Sims, ma'am.

MRS. JEFFERSON: Pleased to meet you, Mistah Sims—

CLARA: Who say you sposeta call in here?

RUDY: Well, we sorta frens with Jack—

CLARA: This here no celebratin party, you know!

MRS. JEFFERSON: Hush, Clara, if they frens with Jack—

CLARA: Why somebody sen us a baseball team here!

RUDY: Mebbe we bess wait outside in de hall, ma'am—

MRS. JEFFERSON: Nothin of the kine! Clara—

CLARA: Ah ain't never seed Jack wid no baseball frens!

(TICK *enters*)

RUDY: Well, Ah nevuh seed him wid you, so we even.

TICK: Don' let her rile you, Rudy. Thanks for comin.

RUDY: Any time, man.

TICK: Got here fass as I could, Miz Jeffson.

MRS. JEFFERSON: Well. You here . . . Come on.

TICK: It ain't good, Miz Jeffson.

SISTER 1: Lawd have mercy.

MRS. JEFFERSON: Come on. Finish up.

TICK: **Twenty-thousand-dollar fine and three years in Joliet.**

SISTER 2: Jesus above.

BROTHER 1: Three years.

CLARA: Why cain't all dem Jew lawyers do nothin! Why cain't—

TICK: Dey got a week ta try appealin on it—

BROTHER 1: Three years.

MRS. JEFFERSON: **Ah die they lock him up!**

SISTER 2: Don' take on, sister—

PASTOR: Bring me them smellin salts—

SISTER 1: Tiny—

MRS. JEFFERSON: No, Ah don' want nothin—

TICK: He do have de week out on bail, Miz Jeffson—dey set it kina heavy but we figgered dey might, an we gonna make it.

MRS. JEFFERSON: A week. Drive him crazy!

TICK: Well, we gotta try an see it don't.

CLARA: That snaky lil wax-face bitch! Where she at now! Where she bloodsuckin now! Oh, Ah'll smoke her out, an, man—

PASTOR: Sister—

CLARA: **What Ah gonna do be worth a hunnerd three yearses!**

MRS. JEFFERSON: Ain't her fault, Clara.

CLARA: She knowd this end-up comin, ain a deaf dumb bline pinhead living din know it, but, Oh, daddy, she joyin hersel so, it so good when it goin! Leave it alone? Oh, but, daddy, Ah loves you!

MRS. JEFFERSON: Could be she do love him, Clara.

CLARA: She WHAT!

MRS. JEFFERSON: **He brung her down once. She din seem too bad.**

TICK: Nice an quiet too.

CLARA: Ah ain't talkin to you! Could be she love him! Why she scat off wid her man in trouble, why she—

PASTOR: Bess unwine dat serpint from you heart, sister—

CLARA: **Love him, my black ass!**

PASTOR: Sister!

MRS. JEFFERSON: (*as* CLARA *returns to kitchen*) Poor gal been frettin so—

(JACK *and* GOLDIE *enter*)

PASTOR: Praise de Lawd an welcome.

JACK: Pastor . . . evvybody . . . good boy, Rudy.

RUDY: Ready fo ya, Jack.

JACK: Fine, no rush . . . hiya, Momma Tiny.

MRS. JEFFERSON: They din hurt you, Jack? You git nuff to eat?

JACK: Sure, Momma.

GOLDIE: **I should feel as good as he does.**

JACK: Whut about you, Momma?

MRS. JEFFERSON: Oh . . .

JACK: Still kina poorly?

MRS. JEFFERSON: It drain me out some, Ah guess.

JACK: Oh, Momma.

BROTHER 2: Hard luck, Jack.

MRS. JEFFERSON: We been prayin an prayin here, son.

JACK: Well . . . de Lawd hear anyone he gonna hear you.

MRS. JEFFERSON: Look like he ain't this time—but He gonna put me on my feet, Ah kin feel it! An Ah gonna help Him, gonna ress up an eat good, an Ah comin down there soon, Jack—

JACK: Momma—

MRS. JEFFERSON: Often as they 'low ya to, you wait an see, bring a big ole picnic basket on my arm—

JACK: No, Momma, listen—

CLARA: (*flinging herself upon him*) Oh, baby, baby, Ah cain't let em clap you in there—

JACK: **What she doin here!**

GOLDIE: That's all we need.

JACK: Git offa me, you! Momma, whut de hell—

MRS. JEFFERSON: Clara come roun when she hear Ah was ailin—

CLARA: Ah been doin fo you momma, Jack—

MRS. JEFFERSON: She tryna menn her ways—

TICK: (*stealing a look out of window*) Jack.

(JACK *looks at him.* HE *nods. Pause*)

JACK: (*to* CLARA) Ah count ten fo you to beat it. One—

CLARA: No!

MRS. JEFFERSON: She been my helpmeet, Jack!

JACK: Sister fine ya a housekeeper!

CLARA: Ah keepin house, baby!

JACK: Ah up to five, girl—

TICK: (*tense. At the window*) Let her be for now, Jack. She in here she cain't spoil it, screamin in the street or somethin.

GOLDIE: (*mopping his face*) That's all we need.

RUDY: Soun like sense, Jack.

MRS. JEFFERSON: Spoil what? Mistah, what these boys up to?

BROTHER 1: Yeah, what goin on here?

CLARA: (*to* TICK *at window*) Whuffo you playin peekaboo wid dat dere automo-bile? (HE *shoos her away*)

PASTOR: (*to* JACK) You ain't about to make things worse, son, are you?

MRS. JEFFERSON: Jack—

JACK: Awright. I gotta truss all you folks now—

PASTOR: Son, however rough it 'pears today—

TICK: Oughta stan by the winder now, Jack. They lookin.

MRS. JEFFERSON: Who? Who lookin?

JACK: 'Tectives in that car, Momma.

MRS. JEFFERSON: Jack—

JACK: Momma, listen—

MRS. JEFFERSON: What they waitin out there for, Mistah Goldie?

GOLDIE: Well, even though Jack is out on bond, you see—

JACK: They worried Ah gonna try an jump mah bail, Momma.

GOLDIE: **They're worried. I'm in hock up to here with this.**

MRS. JEFFERSON: Jack . . . you juss got let out.

JACK: Bess time, Momma. They don' know Ah's ready.

MRS. JEFFERSON: They follerin you, but!

JACK: Thinks they is.

MRS. JEFFERSON: Jack, what if they catches you—

JACK: Won't never get near me! Now, firss thing what Ah do is take my coat off—(*Does so, revealing a raspberry-colored shirt*) then I stan here sorta talkin—"Why heaven sake, no foolin!"—now let em see mah face—(*Looks out*) "Oh, my, it look like rain . . ."—an Ah knows they seen my shirt— **Mm-mm! Don't you wish you had one!** Well, Ah goes on talkin, right? Now over there is Rudy—(RUDY *looks at his watch*) Uh-oh, he checkin his turnip again! They hasta hop on the train soon, you know, Blue Jays playin Montreal nex, ain't you, Rude, gainst de Canada Blacks?

RUDY: Thass right, Jack.

JACK: Less go, fellah—(RUDY *starts peeling off jacket and jersey*) He look mighty fine, ole Rude here, don' he! Not pretty is me, but he near is big an just a half shade blacker an—**Oh, mercy, he got dat shirt on too!** (RUDY *does*)

SISTER 1: Lawd proteck us!

JACK: (*looks out*) "Yeah, it clearin up now—"

GOLDIE: Jack, listen, we should maybe talk it over more—

MRS. JEFFERSON: (*to* GOLDIE) What you trick him inter!

GOLDIE: It's his idea, believe me—

JACK: It be awright, Momma! Rudy spen de aftuhnoon by the winder an Ah go rollin cross de border with de Jays!

BROTHER 2: They fine you out, Jack—

JACK: Naw! I put on Rudy's cap an his jacket? Stick in the middle of his boys? Who all fine me! An who lookin? **You hear that sayin how all niggers look alike!** Ain't that so, team?

PASTOR: But, son, you fogittin we frens with that Canada! I mean, we's hardly a diffrunt place—

TICK: Fore they cotton to it, man, we on dat ole boat to Englin. Right?

GOLDIE: Right, right.

JACK: It all fixed, Momma!

MRS. JEFFERSON: All what fixed ain't gotta juss happen—

PASTOR: Serious offense to go floutin de law, Jack! I know they done you real hard but, son, it gonna hang ovuh you long as—

JACK: Look! What hang gonna hang but Ah ain't hangin with it! Ah done my kickin roun this country, Ah serve my one nights and my thirty days too once, an Ah ain't gonna rot like no log no three years! Or be comin out broke as Ah is now either! Ah in the prime of mah life! Ah wanna live like Ah got to, wanna make me some money again, wanna fight! **Ah got my turn to be Champeen of the World an Ah takin my turn! Ah stayin whut Ah am, wherever Ah has to do it! The world ain't curled up into no forty-eight states here!**

MRS. JEFFERSON: Praise de Lawd for lightin a way fo my boy! Fogive me Ah say Ah didden love you, Jesus!

JACK: (*moving to her*) Thassit, Momma—

MRS. JEFFERSON: (*to* BROTHERS *and* PASTOR) Well?

BROTHERS & PASTOR: (*worried*) Amen . . .

GOLDIE: **She could put in a word for me too, here.**

RUDY: (*taking his place at the window*) Better move it, man.

JACK: Right. (*Pulls on* RUDY'S *jersey*)

GOLDIE: Oh, boy.

JACK: You folks stay here till we gone, OK? Then start runnin in an out like, keep em busy watchin—

CLARA: Oh, take me with you, honey—

JACK: (*pulls on a jacket*) Don't you cross me now—

CLARA: Ah go meet you, baby! Any place!

JACK: You know the score, girl.

CLARA: Please!

JACK: (*buttoning up*) Fit awright?

GOLDIE: Yeah, beautiful.

CLARA: She comin to ya, ain't she! That where she at!

JACK: Hope you gettin to that game on time, Rudy—

CLARA: You ain't meetin that bitch! I turn you in firss—(*Runs at the door*)

TICK: Hole her—

CLARA: (*shaking loose from him*) JACK GONNA—(*Struggles with* SISTERS *at the door*)

SISTER 1: Stop her mouf up—

CLARA: HE RUNNIN FFFF—(*Stopping her mouth,* THEY *drag her from the door, kicking*)

GOLDIE: Oh, boy—

BROTHER 1: Make some noise!

SISTER 2: Sit on her—

PASTOR: "Look ovuh, Beulah—"

BROTHER 2: Which—?

PASTOR: Ready—

MRS. JEFFERSON: No "Beulah" now, sen up a glad one—

SISTER 1: Quick, she bitin me—

MRS. JEFFERSON: Sing, chillun—

ALL: (*but* CLARA, *on whom the three largest* SISTERS *are sitting*)
Just to talk to Jesus
Oh, what a joy de-vine
Ah kin feel de lectric
Movin on de line,
All wired up by God de Father
For his lovin own,
Put a call to Jesus
On the Royal Telephone—

JACK: (*over the singing*) Here, where that Jew's-harp—(*Finds it*) Plung on it, Rudy, it cover you face up—(*Tosses it to him.* RUDY *plays.* JACK *moves among them*) Good luck—thank you —thank you—see you soon—you too—don't worry—Thank you, Momma Tiny—Get well, darlin, try, please try—Say you come an see me—good-bye, my momma, good-bye, my sweetheart—

(MRS. JEFFERSON *nods and sings right on, clapping to the beat, and with* GOLDIE *mopping his face,* CLARA *kicking and crying,* RUDY *twanging and* ALL THE REST *in full chorus,* JACK *puts on his cap and disappears with the* JAYS)

ALL:
   Angel operators
   Waitin for you call,
   Central up in heaven,
   Take no time at all,
   Ring, and God will answer
   In his happy tone,
   Put a call to Jesus
   On the Royal Telephone.

CURTAIN ACT ONE

Some dozen chairs facing a large desk are arranged for the hearing about to take place. As the scene begins, SIX MEN *and* ONE WOMAN, *all middle-aged and soberly dressed, are seating themselves. From a door opposite,* EUBANKS, *assistant to the Undersecretary, enters chatting with* TREACHER, JACK'S *solicitor. Enter* JACK, ELLIE, GOLDIE, TICK.

TREACHER: Ah, good morning—

EUBANKS: I'll go and fetch Sir William. (*Goes*)

JACK: Mornin, evvybody . . . Mornin, Miz Kimball . . . How you today, Mac . . . ? (THEY *stare straight ahead*) **Muss be de Wax Museum took a branch here.**

TREACHER: Over there, please, Jack.

GOLDIE: And let Mr. Treacher do the talking, understand?

TREACHER: Yes, thank you.

JACK: (*to* ELLIE) We straighten dis out, hon.

ELLIE: Well, I hope so.

JACK: Feelin kina edgy, huh.

ELLIE: (*takes his hand*) No.

TICK: **Ah does.**

EUBANKS: (*entering*) Sir William Griswold.

JACK: (*to* ELLIE) Hey, you breakin mah han!

(SIR WILLIAM *enters.* GOLDIE, TICK, *and the* WOMAN *stand up*)

SIR WILLIAM: Good morning—no, no need to rise, thank you. (*Sits at desk*) Yes . . . Now, then. Allegations have been made to us concerning the possible undesirability of an alien person's continued visit here. **We have of course our own book of rules on the subject, and normally—**

COATES: With due respect, Sir William, I'm amazed that you find this necessary.

SIR WILLIAM: Mr.—?

COATES: Coates.

SIR WILLIAM: (*to* EUBANKS) Representing?

EUBANKS: British Vigilance Board.

COATES: Can you really be debating this? A convicted criminal, a fugitive from justice—

TREACHER: My client's conviction was known to the authorities. He was admitted at their discretion.

SIR WILLIAM: That is true, Mr. Coates.

COATES: And our discreet authorities are helpless to correct their initial error, is that what you imply, sir?

SIR WILLIAM: I implied nothing, I'm sure.

COATES: Your official silence indeed implies something! Like official license for breaches of the peace, for moral deficiency flaunted at the public—

JACK: Now wait—Ah ain't flung no fish at no public!

COATES: I beg your—

TICK: Jack, you hush up—

SIR WILLIAM: Gentlemen, please—

MRS. KIMBALL: (*the* WOMAN) I'll tell them what you did do, you great flash nig-nog!

EUBANKS: Madam, really—

GOLDIE: Don't you talk like that, lady—

COATES: Mrs. Kimball here—

MRS. KIMBALL: (*to* COATES) Do I speak my piece now—?

EUBANKS: Mr. Coates has the—

COATES: No, go on, Mrs. Kimball.

MRS. KIMBALL: I rented him my luxury maisonette, your honor, Ten Portman Square, and not many would rent to them, believe you me, a black and white job to boot, but I thought they at least was married, which they wasn't, and I thought she being white they'd be clean, which they wasn't, and I thought maybe them being lovebirds like they are they'd settle down early nights—nothing of the kind! Parties, champagne, nigger piano playing—mind you, I like a bit of music, but I never, all night, screaming up the stairwell. Oh, yes, I'd see them through the door when I went to shut em up, doing their dirty dances in there—**Turkey Trot and all the rest of them colored steps!**

COATES: The damage to Mrs. Kimball's flat, Sir William, was appraised at nearly four hundred pounds.

MRS. KIMBALL: Yes, that's right! Vases, chippendale, can't replace it neither—**and rubbish all over too, the filthy ape!** Undesirable!

TREACHER: The amount has been paid in full, Sir William.

SIR WILLIAM: Who is next, Mr. Coates?

COATES: Inspector Wainwright.

EUBANKS: Metropolitan Police.

WAINWRIGHT: (*reading from notebook*) November ninth. Charged with using obscene language on Coventry Street. Fine, two pounds. November fifteenth. Charged with causing a crowd to collect. Fine, fifty shillings. Fined a further five pounds for contempt of court.

SIR WILLIAM: (*to* JACK) Why the fine for contempt, may I ask.

JACK: Well, de judge he yell, Ah fine you fifty shillins! So Ah says, Look, dat crowd's still collectin so maybe you better take a hundred off me.

WAINWRIGHT: November twenty-fifth—

SIR WILLIAM: (*to* COATES) If the police offenses are all of this nature—

COATES: You may skip to January third, Wainwright.

WAINWRIGHT: January third. Charged with assault on Mr. M. Bratby.

TREACHER: The charge has been dropped, Sir William.

COATES: Sir, when a man trained in the use of his fists—

JACK: No, Ah juss shoved him—(*To* BRATBY) Whut you tell this man, Mac?

SIR WILLIAM: You are—?

BRATBY: M. Bratby.

EUBANKS: Olympia Sporting Club.

BRATBY: Jefferson came to us proposing that we match him. We had been unwilling to associate ourselves with him—we expressed this position—he became unruly—

COATES: Attacked you, you mean!

TREACHER: The affair has been settled, Mr. Jefferson's apology—

COATES: Yes, all the affairs are settled, the popular press delightedly reports them, and nightly in the music halls they are dealt with as a joke! Is any of this desirable? This, when disruption is the order of the day, with the ground we stand on undermined by socialists, atheists, anarchists, with anarchy not merely a word but a man with a bomb in a public building—

SIR WILLIAM: Mr. Coates—

COATES: And you're amused, sir, when this lady refers to these dances coming into vogue since this man's arrival here, but read your Plato, Sir William, read your Plato—

SIR WILLIAM: I say—

COATES: "New modes of music herald upheavals of state," sir—

SIR WILLIAM: Now really, Mr. Coates, I have seen the Turkey Trot—

COATES: Let me remind you of the waltz, Sir William—

SIR WILLIAM: The waltz?

COATES: The first waltz, sir—

SIR WILLIAM: Are you asking me to dance—?

TREACHER: Sir William, may I venture—

JACK: No, Ah kin talk.

SIR WILLIAM: Yes, please. Go ahead.

JACK: Ah come over as a prizefighter, sir. Figgered Ah could fight Billy Wells here or Jeannette, an make me mah livin here the way Ah knows how. But we coulden git no decent match fix up, so Ah was juss gittin fat, and kickin up and fussin people. Now, Ah guess Ah shouldn've, cause whut Ah am, you know, cullud Ah mean, some folks here think is a freak anyway, but it took me some time gittin use to bein here, an Ah'm sorry bout all these stories they brung in, an whut Ah wanna say is, we like it here fine now, and now Lord Londsale done set me up a match, Ah'll git trainin and fightin an we won't have no mo rumpus.

SIR WILLIAM: Well, Mr. Coates, as I see this at the moment, the American legalities are none of our concern, the breaches of the peace you've cited are trivial, the man's moral character deficient perhaps, by Queen Victoria's standards—**but she of course is gone now**—and as to the palaver in the press and music halls these are liberties we simply have to bear—think of them as part of the White Man's Burden. So unless Mr. Jefferson commits a crime of some sort—which I hope none of you will tempt him to further—I do not see— You have something to add?

COATES: I should like to correct Mr. Jefferson's assumption that he does indeed have a match on, Sir William.

JACK: Whut you talkin bout, Ah sign up wid him dere— (*Points to* BRATBY) **fightin Albert Lynch on March de eighteenth—**

SIR WILLIAM: Is this relevant, Mr. Coates—

COATES: Oh, I think so. Bratby?

BRATBY: Two weeks ago, at Lord Londsdale's persuasion, we proposed this match, and Jefferson accepted. It now appears, however, that the London County Council refuses to issue a license for this fight. And enquiries indicate this difficulty elsewhere.

TREACHER: Refused the license on what grounds?

COATES: Mr. Farlow?

FARLOW: I should say that Mr. Coates has already expressed the Council's position.

JACK: Goldie, how the hell—

TICK: Sit easy there, baby—

COATES: This man entered England with the stated purpose of pursuing his career as a pugilist. Now, what, sir, are the grounds for his remaining in England if this career of his does simply not exist here!

(JACK *stands,* ELLIE *holds him by the hand*)

SIR WILLIAM: Please sit down, sir. (*To the others*) I shall make no comment on the principles or motives operating among you. I shall only inform you that an alien is free to change his means of livelihood, **he may take up any—**

JACK: OK. Les go.

TICK: De guy still—

JACK: Up!

(ELLIE *gets up and* TICK *gets up*)

SIR WILLIAM: (*to* JACK) It is understood, I hope, that—

JACK: Come on, Goldie—(*To* SIR WILLIAM) Ah thank you fo you time, sir, an stickin up fo me—

SIR WILLIAM: I'm really very sorry—

JACK: You scuse us now, please—(*To* TREACHER) See you, Mr. Treacher—

ELLIE: Jack—

COATES: (*to* TREACHER) Your client will be leaving the country, I take it.

JACK: Yeah, man, you take it. It's all yours.

(BLACKOUT. *Boat whistle, train whistle, another boat whistle, crowd, band playing.* LIGHTS UP *on*—)

---

scene two

A customs shed, Le Havre.

At one side, with the BAND, *a welcoming* CROWD: OFFICIALS, PRESS, *etc., some waving small tricolors. At the other side* TWO UNIFORMED INSPECTORS, *beyond them a sign:* DOUANE. *Some* PORTERS *hurry past them, wheeling trunks, and a* CHEER *goes up behind them. Followed by his* ENTOURAGE, *greeting the* CROWD *with hands clasped triumphantly over his head, appears* KLOSSOWSKI, *a Polish heavyweight. The* PHOTOGRAPHERS' *flares commence, and continue through the scene. The* BAND *stops playing as* KLOSSOWSKI *meets the* OFFICIALS *and* PRESS, *shaking hands and embracing all around.*

OFFICIAL: Bienvenue encore à la France, Monsieur Klossowski!

CROWD: Bravo, Klossowski! Bienvenue! Bonne arrivée!

KLOSSOWSKI: Merci, merci, mes amis, mille mercis—

PRESSMAN 1: Alors, vous êtes prêt pour votre grand combat avec le noir Jefferson?

KLOSSOWSKI: Oho, monsieur—je suis absolument—

PRESSMAN 1: Confiant?

KLOSSOWSKI: C'est ça! **Con-fi-dent! Je m'excuse que mon français est terrible—**

CROWD: Mais non, mais non!

PRESSMAN 3: Mais vous n'êtes pas hésitant à faire la boxe avec le champion du monde? Un petit peu?

KLOSSOWSKI: Hésitant! Ha, ha, ha!

CROWD: Bravo, Klossowski!

KLOSSOWSKI: Écoutez—Je boxai à Buenos Aires avec Paco Flores! Zut! Zut! Zut! Trois rounds, je gagne! Je boxai à Rio Pereira! Zut! Frappe! Deux rounds, je gagne! Je boxai en Afrique avec un noir gigantesque là—Zut! Boom! **Pas de conteste, messieurs!** Et cette Jefferson, qui c'est, qui c'est? Oh, champion du monde, oui, lalala—mais il n'a pas boxé pour longtemps! (*Miming it*) Il boit le whiskey, il fume les cigares, il est gros, il êtes lourde, il vit comme un—un—

PRESSMAN 1: Cochon? (*Laughter*)

KLOSSOWSKI: C'est ça! (*Laughter*) Non, messieurs, c'est pas la vie du boxeur! (*Mimes it all*) Moi, je cours chaque jour trente kilomètres, même à la bateau—oui! Je saute à la corde: cent fois! Je boxe l'ombre: une heure! Petit sac, vingt minutes! Des gymnastiques, quarante minutes, deux fois, matin et soir, et bain chaud! Douche froid! Forte massage après midi, mange bien, dix heures sommeil—(*Laughter*) Vous pensez que j'éxagère? Attendez le combat Jefferson—(*Acts it out*) et zut! Zut! Gauche à l'estomac! Droite à la tête! Gauche encore! Zut! Frappe! Boom! Dix! Voilà—**vous verrez!**

(*Cheering,* THEY *hoist him on their shoulders, the* BAND *strikes up, and he is borne off as* LIGHTS FADE: *new* CROWD SOUND *gradually replacing cheering, an arena* CROWD, *distant.* LIGHTS UP *on—*)

scene three

Jack's dressing room at the Vel d'Hiver arena, Paris.

JACK *is sitting on table.* TICK *taping his hands.* ELLIE. *A French* HANDLER *busy with towels, sponge, salts, etc.*

TICK: Keep breathin deep, champ, nice an slow now.

JACK: Ah knows howta breathe.

TICK: Gonna finish off dat Polack like a chicken dinner!

JACK: Hurry it up, huh.

TICK: Ain even gonna muss you wool up on him!

JACK: Don' talk like that fronna her.

ELLIE: Jack, don't be silly—

JACK: An when you start callin me "champ" anyway?

TICK: Hey, come on. See if that too tight now.

  (GOLDIE *enters*)

ELLIE: Full house?

GOLDIE: Girlie, they're hangin from the rafters.

JACK: Water bottle, Tick. Wanna rinse.

GOLDIE: You OK?

JACK: Why you keep askin me?

GOLDIE: So what, so I'm askin!

JACK: You worried bout somethin? What you worrying bout!

TICK: **Man, dat Polack sure in for it tonight.**

GOLDIE: Tick, for chrissake—

TICK: (*to* HANDLER) Uh—hey, Jim, where that O bottle gone to?

HANDLER: Comment?

TICK: The O. You know, O?

HANDLER: Le—Ah—

TICK: No, the O—

HANDLER: La bouteille!

TICK: Mistah who?

JACK: Never mine—

HANDLER: Non?

TICK: Yeah, the O!

HANDLER: De l'eau! (*Produces it*)

TICK: Attaboy! **See? Juss be patient with em.**

(*Gives it to* JACK, *who gargles and spits*)

JACK: Bad tase in there, thassall.

GOLDIE: (*to* TICK) Coupla more minutes.

TICK: (*to* JACK) Put em up, baby, we better warm up some. Huh? OK?

JACK: Ah warm up inside there with the man.

TICK: Aw, be good now! Ah ain't gonna get you winded—

ELLIE: Tick!

JACK: You don' haveta tell me what wind Ah ain't got.

TICK: No, man, Ah mean—

JACK: Ah know what shape is an when Ah ain in it. Ah know when gettin in it's a waste a my good time too! **Ah don' gotta train to take no fifth-rate geechee—**

GOLDIE: Jack, who says different—

JACK: Thass who Ah fightin here, ain it!

GOLDIE: It's the best they got around here, Jack—

JACK: Hit him one an shovel up the money, right? Jump in with the big gole belt, right?

TICK: (*sings*)
**Niggers is evil
White folks too.
So glad Ah'm a Chinaman,
Don' know whut to do.**

(PROMOTER *enters*)

PROMOTER: If you please, messieurs.

ELLIE: I'll go in to my seat now.

JACK: Honey—

ELLIE: (*kisses him*) Good luck, darlin—

JACK: Do me a favor. Stay here.

ELLIE: Oh, Jack.

JACK: Nothin in there you wanna see.

PROMOTER: Come along, please, messieurs—(*To* HANDLER) vite, vite—(*To* JACK) But, oh, Monsieur Jefferson, the smile, the famous smile—You will not deny to our public the smile!

JACK: No, Ah got it on me.

PROMOTER: Ha, ha, very good.

TICK: **We won't be too long.**

(THEY *leave.* ELLIE *sits. A few seconds go by and the* CROWD ROAR *increases in volume.* ELLIE *stands, wanders aimlessly, spies a newspaper, tries to read it, puts it down. Over the* CROWD NOISES *the* ANNOUNCER'S VOICE *is heard, incoherent.* ELLIE *folds a towel, a jersey, sits again.* SMITTY *enters*)

SMITTY: Hi there, Miss Bachman.

ELLIE: Hello—

SMITTY: Smith, *Evening Mirror.* Smitty?

ELLIE: Oh, yes.

102   THE GREAT WHITE HOPE

SMITTY: Mind if I—

ELLIE: Aren't you here for the fight?

SMITTY: Well, the boys'll dope me in. He's at it again, that's the main thing.

ELLIE: Yes.

SMITTY: I've missed him, Old Jack. How is he, anyway?

ELLIE: Fine.

SMITTY: Sure is looking good! Oh, a little moody—

ELLIE: A little.

SMITTY: That'll pass, don't let it get you down. Part of it's all this moving around.

ELLIE: Yes.

SMITTY: Once you're not, and settle in somewhere—(*A* ROAR) There they go! You know what I mean?

ELLIE: Yes.

SMITTY: Makes all the difference.

ELLIE: Probably.

SMITTY: Sure—and how long can it be!

ELLIE: I don't know, really.

SMITTY: Bet you can't wait, huh? Either of you!

ELLIE: We talk about it.

SMITTY: Yeah, what a feeling—like to have a little nest here, do you think?

ELLIE: We haven't made any—(A ROAR. SHE *shivers*)

SMITTY: Listen to em! No idea? (SHE *shakes her head*) Christ, that must be hard on you now . . . hm? (*No reply*) Well, leave that all to Jack! As long as you rest and keep your strength up—(SHE *faces him.* A ROAR) I've had four myself and let me tell you—

ELLIE: Go away, will you.

SMITTY: Ah, be a sport, when's it going to be?

ELLIE: It's not. Go away.

SMITTY: I mean, you were looking so peaked the other day, I had a hunch—(A ROAR. SHE *turns away*) Say, don't get sore! Look, the folks back home—

ELLIE: I told you: no!

SMITTY: **I hate to let you down, folks!**

(A ROAR)

ELLIE: Now, please—

(A ROAR)

SMITTY: Something else, maybe? Wedding bells? Homesick? Hear from your family?

(A ROAR. SHE *covers her ears, shuddering*)

ELLIE: Oh, it's never—

SMITTY: Are you feeling OK, Miss Bachman?

ELLIE: Yes—

(A ROAR)

SMITTY: He's dishing it out, he's not getting it—

ELLIE: Please—(A ROAR. SHE *bites her hand*)

SMITTY: You don't look too hot—Here, take a swallow—(SHE *shakes her head. The* ROARING *is continuous now,* SMITTY *is nearly shouting*) How long do you think you can take it, anyway, living like this! It has to burn you out, Miss Bachman, can't you see that? Burn you out! You're not as tough as he is, you know, you can't just go on—

(*The noise has turned to* ANGRY BOOS *and* CATCALLS; RUNNING FEET, *a* BELL CLANGING. SHOUTS *nearby:* "Sauvage! Assassin!" JACK, TICK, GOLDIE, *and the* PROMOTER *burst in, blood smears on* JACK's *gloves and chest. Sounds of* POLICE SCUFFLING *in the corridor*)

GOLDIE: God, why'd you keep—

PROMOTER: Quickly, please!

ELLIE: What happened—Jack—

JACK: He'll come out of it—

GOLDIE: Grab that bag—

JACK: It's all right, honey—

TICK: **Yeah—just!**

ELLIE: No—

PROMOTER: This way, please—

GOLDIE: Dress in the car, Jack—

PROMOTER: I beg of you!

JACK: Come on, honey. I'm sorry, I'm sorry.

(*Leads* HER *off*, LIGHTS *and* SHOUTS FADING. DARKNESS)

scene four

Pop Weaver's office, New York.

The darkened office suite of POP WEAVER, *promoter. In the flickering light of the film* THEY *are watching sit* POP, CAP'N DAN, *and* FRED, *formerly* BRADY'S *manager.*

CAP'N DAN: How much you say he weighs, Fred?

FRED: Two thirty-seven. He's six foot five . . . watch it! Mommer!

POP: Not bad, Cap'n Dan, eh?

FRED: Wait, here's Vancouver two weeks ago—hold on—there's my boy! The one on the left.

CAP'N DAN: You couldn't exactly miss him, Fred.

FRED: Rushes straight in—there! I don't wanna brag, but when that kid first—(*The film breaks; only the beam continues*) Ah, for crying out loud!

VOICE: (*offstage*) Won't take a minute.

FRED: So? Waddaya say! **If that's no White Hope I'm Queen Pocahontas.**

POP: He's the right stuff, Dan. Maybe a little raw yet—

FRED: Fresh, fresh is what he is! Big, clean, strong, a real farmboy! They're waiting on their knees for something like him! (*Silence.* THEY *stare at the blank screen*)

FRED: (*calling out*) How about it there!

CAP'N DAN: I don't think we need to see any more, Pop.

POP: Lights, please, Harry. (*The room is lit*) Well, you tell me, Dan. You want me to promote it, I'm ready to promote it, anytime, anywhere.

FRED: (*to* CAP'N DAN) Right!

POP: What do you think, Dan?

CAP'N DAN: I think he's a full-grown polar bear, myself.

FRED: Well, we have to send over somebody, don't we? The papers are hollerin, all the old bull again—**Honest, it's gettin like Remember the Maine here!**

CAP'N DAN: Oh, he fills the bill all right. But say we do send him over, and the black boy does it again, Fred. Then where are we.

POP: You won't ever have it on a plate, Dan, you know.

CAP'N DAN: Pop, Fred. Let me tell you a secret. The next White Hope is the one who gets the belt back. Not means to, or almost does, or gets half-killed trying: he takes it, he finishes right on his feet, with a big horizontal nigger down for good there.

POP: What do you mean, Dan? Is it yes or no.

CAP'N DAN: I'd like you to meet a friend of mine, Pop. (*Calls*) Mr. Dixon there yet?

VOICE: (*offstage*) Yeah!

CAP'N DAN: Come on in. (*Enter* DIXON) Pop Weaver. Fred.

POP: Have a chair, Mr. Dixon.

DIXON: (*sits*) Thanks. (*To* CAP'N DAN) All right?

CAP'N DAN: Oh, we're hopeful, I think. (THEY *laugh*) Dixon here is with the Bureau in Washington. Like you might expect, they have Mr. Jefferson on their minds, too. I've been down there, we've had some ideas—you explain it to them, son.

DIXON: When a man beats us out like this, we—the law, that is—suffer in prestige, and that's pretty serious. How people regard the law is part of its effectiveness, it can't afford to look foolish, and this applies especially now to our Negro population. I don't mean just the ones who always flout the law, and seeing their hero doing it in style act up more than usual—those are police concerns, not ours. But though you may not be aware of it yet, a very large, very black migration is in progress. They're coming from the fields down there and filling up the slums, trouble's starting in Europe, and our mills and factories have work for them now. And I'm talking of hundreds of thousands, maybe millions soon—**millions of ignorant Negroes, rapidly massing together, their leanings, their mood, their outlook, suddenly no longer regulated by the little places they come from—situations have arisen already.** We cannot allow the image of this man to go on impressing and exciting these people.

POP: I'm only a sports promoter, Mr. Dixon.

CAP'N DAN: He read the writing on the door, Pop. Go on.

DIXON: If this position he enjoys were to be lost, through the outcome of his next engagement, let's say, the effect of this would be so much in our interest that we would be disposed to reconsider his sentence.

POP: You'd make it worth his while not to win the fight, you mean.

DIXON: I think I've said what I mean, Mr. Weaver.

CAP'N DAN: (*to* DIXON) What's the furthest you can go.

DIXON: We'd reduce it to a year, of which he'd serve six months, preferred treatment, best facilities, etcetera. **We're willing to make this as attractive as possible.**

FRED: I say my kid can beat him fair and square!

POP: Don't ride it, Fred.

FRED: Look, if you won't promote it, I'll hop on a boat with him and find someone who will!

CAP'N DAN: You don't want to do that, Fred.

FRED: What am I, a—

CAP'N DAN: Fred. I'm tellin you as a friend.

FRED: **I just don't like it.**

POP: It goes against me too, Dan.

CAP'N DAN: And against me too! I don't have to make anybody no speech here about how good I feel working something crooked! None of us like it—**we wouldn't be the men we are if we did, or be where we are! I know it's lousy!** But we got a situation here needs a little bending, the man's tried to tell you how serious it is, they're bending with it, I'm bending with it, who are you to sit there and say it goes against you, or you either, on your pedestal here!

POP: What about the champ, though, Dan?

FRED: He'll never buy it! Or my kid either, he's straight outa Sunday school, he's—

CAP'N DAN: Shut up, Fred—nobody has to tell your kid a thing! And Jack, well, after that last one, nobody there'll fight him any more, he's down to giving exhibitions, peanuts—

POP: But serving six months, Dan—

CAP'N DAN: It can't be much worse than killing the six months. And he'll step out a free man—**all that fight money! See all his pals!** Besides, his ole mammy ain't been too good, he'll want to see her before she goes. Sure he'll take it.

POP: Dan, why not ask Weiler or Michel to set it up, someone on the spot there?

CAP'N DAN: I'm asking you, Pop. (*Pause*)

POP: (*to* DIXON) You can't put that deal in writing, can you mister?

DIXON: Sorry, Pop. I wasn't even here. (*Pause*)

POP: What the hell, Fred. We'll balance it out on the one after this. Everything back on the gold standard, right?

FRED: OK, OK.

DIXON: (*rising*) Well, thank you, gentlemen—(THEY *all rise*)

CAP'N DAN: And we thank you!

POP: I wouldn't count on results straight off, though.

DIXON: Oh, I think the country can hold up a little while. (THEY *laugh,* DIXON *waves them silent*) Excuse me—**You seem to be indignant, sir. Yes, I heard you. We have that all the time from people like you, that old Machiavelli crap. Look into it further, sir. But not in here, or at home. Give it some thought next time you're alone on the streets late at night.** (*To* CAP'N DAN) I'll be in touch with you.

(LIGHTS FADE. BLACKOUT. MUSIC: *German street band, distant.* LIGHTS UP *on—*)

scene five

A sidewalk café, Berlin.

JACK, TICK, *four drunken* GERMAN OFFICERS *with them.* JACK *Indian-wrestling the largest,* OFFICER 4, *on the stein-covered table, as the other three encourage their comrade.*

OFFICER 1: Jetzt!

OFFICER 2: Kraft, Hans—

OFFICER 3: Ringe!

OFFICER 4: Kann nicht!

OFFICER 1: Nein!

OFFICER 4: Himmelsgott!

OFFICER 2: Ja!

(JACK *begins to bear his arm down*)

OFFICER 3: Aber, Hans—

OFFICER 1: Nein!

OFFICER 4: Mutter!

OFFICER 2: Halt—

OFFICER 1: Nein—

OFFICER 3: Nein, nein—

ALL: A-a-a-h!

OFFICER 1: Wunderbar! **Herrlich!** Mein herr, you are the triumph!

JACK: Well, thanks for stoppin roun, boys—

OFFICER 2: **Wir müssen die Fahne vom Regiment präsentieren!**

OFFICER 1: He says we must present to you the flag of our regiment!

JACK: Oh, cain't take that, ahma Mercan citizen—

TICK: You buy some tickets fo de show, dassall—

OFFICER 4: (*offering his arm*) Bitte—again, please—

JACK: Tomorrow, buddy, you done wore me out.

  (ALL OFFICERS *laugh*)

TICK: We see you all tomorrow, huh?

OFFICER 1: (*picking up stein*) Kameradschaft!

  (*The* OTHERS *follow suit*)

JACK: (*standing*) Camera shaft, OK.

TICK: **Lawd, the drinkin sure hard on the feet here.**

OFFICER 4: Wir müssen ihm etwas geben!

ALL: Ja! Ja!

OFFICER 1: Mein herr, we go provide for you the suitable memento.

JACK: Great, be lookin out for ya.

TICK: Weenersane, weenersane.

ALL OFFICERS: (*leaving*) Hop, hop, hop, hop . . .

JACK: (*yawning and stretching*) O mah bones, whut you after.

TICK: Wanna go back to the hotel?

JACK: (*sits*) Naw. Nothin doin there. You ready fo anuther?

TICK: Ah better pass. (*Sips*) Wonder how they make it brew up so heavy. You think they mix a egg in or whut?

JACK: Beats me, man. Puttin me to sleep, though.

TICK: Well, thass whut they does after lunch here, right?

JACK: No, man, that were someplace else.

(ELLIE *enters with* RAGOSY, *an impresario*)

RAGOSY: Ah, Meester Jafferson—

JACK: Whut you bring him for—?

RAGOSY: Such delights again to see you—

JACK: Now ain Ah tole you, mistah—

RAGOSY: Ragosy, excuse—(*Gives card*)

114   THE GREAT WHITE HOPE

ELLIE: He just tagged along, Jack—

RAGOSY: I am patient rewarded!

TICK: Which one wuz he?

JACK: Huh . . . lemme think now . . . You ain't the one wanted me to team up with a circus—

RAGOSY: Please?

JACK: An it wusn't you pushin me to start a restrunt with him—

RAGOSY: No, no—

JACK: Or the artiss guy gonna hire me an do me in black cement?

RAGOSY: But you recall Ragosy!

TICK: Man, he that Hungrarian!

JACK: Oh, yeah, thassright—

(WAITER *enters*)

RAGOSY: Please, not speak additional word, I supply first champagne—(*To* WAITER) Abräumen, bitte! (*To* JACK) Wait, not to trust here, I consult myself—sit! (*Goes in*)

JACK: (*to* ELLIE) Why dinya sen him up ta Goldie, Goldie brush him!

ELLIE: He wasn't there, he had to go out.

TICK: Oh yeah? Something movin?

ELLIE: Just meeting that reporter.

JACK: Smitty?

ELLIE: Yes, he rang up.

JACK: Whut he doin here?

TICK: Must be he onna job an he sayin hello.

JACK: Nothin goin on here.

TICK: You ain't the only item in the paper, bighead.

RAGOSY: (*reentering with champagne;* WAITER *sets glasses*) See, from my own hands! I take it the privilege—Champion, lovely friends—

TICK: **Ready wid de pumps, men.**

RAGOSY: Oh, Meester Jafferson! It pains in my heart these nights attending you. I count there the people and I make totality: **one-quarter business!** you do not divert!

JACK: Mebbe Ah oughta wear a bone through mah nose.

RAGOSY: No, no! For the true fisticuff with bleedings they come, but now you are not doing, you must look otherwise. I implore again myself, let Ragosy be devising the spectacle to you— Song! Dancing! **Sentiment!** The name is on you still like a diamond, my friend, only let make necessary light and then, then—

JACK: (*leaping up: buck and wing*) **Out in San Francisco where de weather's fair Dey have a dance out dere—**

RAGOSY: Ah, aha—

JACK: **Dey call the Grizzly Bear, All your other lovin' dances don't compare—**†

ELLIE: Jack, please stop it.

JACK: What?

ELLIE: Can't you just tell him no and—

JACK: Ah tell him whut Ah wants to, hon—

ELLIE: Jack, we're in the street—

JACK: An where Ah wants to an how, hear?

TICK: Baby, all she sayin—

JACK: Who ass you! (*To* ELLIE) Talk to me bout streets. If you so goddam tetchy bout people lookin you ain't even oughta be here!

ELLIE: I don't like them looking when you're this way—

JACK: No? Well, me neither! But Ah's stuck widdit an you ain't, so any time you wanna—where you goin!

RAGOSY: (*rising*) Oh, Madam, I sincerely—

JACK: (*to* ELLIE) Git you ass back on there! Man bought champagne—

RAGOSY: Please, Meester Jafferson—

JACK: You siddown too! (RAGOSY *does*)

ELLIE: I'll be in the room.

JACK: Yeah, then you say you sicka waitin roun hotels!

ELLIE: I never said that.

JACK: You givin out you misery so hard you don' haveta! You juss don' like nothin no more!

ELLIE: I won't answer you—

JACK: Dassit, give it out!

ELLIE: What do you want, Jack!

JACK: **Don' like nothin!**

ELLIE: (*going*) Excuse me, please—

JACK: You siddown here, girl—

TICK: Let her go, man, she got the Fear again—

JACK: (*calling after her*) ELLIE!

TICK: (*following*) Ah walk her on back—

(NOISE *of rhythmical clanging and shouting*)

JACK: Tell that Goldie Ah wants him, hear!

TICK: (*looking in direction of noise*) Say—

JACK: Git! (*Holds ears*) Oh, them heavy-foot bastuds.

TICK: (*going*) **He turnin meaner than a red hyena.**

JACK: (*toasting* RAGOSY) Happy days, mistah—

RAGOSY: Prosit, prosit, and I eagerly to hope we—(RAGOSY *slips off as the* FOUR OFFICERS *gaily return: one is beating on dust-*

bin lid with a chair leg, two of the others frog-march between them a very black young NEGRO, *who struggles violently*)

NEGRO: Lassen mir! Lassen mir absteigen!

JACK: Hey—

OFFICER 1: So, we bring you as we promise—halt!

OFFICER 4: Einen Schwarzen Kameraden—(*Laughing,* THEY *dump* NEGRO. JACK *helps him up*)

JACK: Here, lemme duss you off—

OFFICER 2: Is suitable, nein?

NEGRO: Mutig Soldaten spielen wie Kinder! (*Jeers and laughter*)

JACK: Don' rile em, man—

NEGRO: Again, bitte?

JACK: Whut—where the hell you from, anyway?

OFFICER 1: Where! He must ask! (*Gales of laughter*)

NEGRO: Afrika.

OFFICER 2: Boomboomboom!

OFFICER 4: Crucrucru!

OFFICER 3: **Authentick, ja!**

JACK: Oh, Jesus.

OFFICER 1: Here, you observe? (*Points to scars on* NEGRO's *face.* JACK *gasps. More laughter*)

NEGRO: Ja. Iss tribe mark.

OFFICER 2: Walawalawala!

NEGRO: Here iss custom more large. (*Makes gesture of dueling scar.* OFFICER 4 *goes for him*)

OFFICER 4: Scheissfarbiger Hund—

OFFICER 2: (*as other* OFFICERS *tussle with* OFFICER 4, *restraining him*) Nein, Hans, nein—

JACK: Go siddown there, Jim—

NEGRO: Please?

JACK: (*pushing him toward table*) Move—(*Going to struggling* OFFICERS) Well, much obliged, fellahs, thass zackly what Ah wanted—(OFFICER 4 *breaks away,* JACK *catches him by arm*) Hey, Hands, you know this one? (*Stands with him toe to toe*)

OFFICERS 1, 2, 3: Ah!

OFFICER 2: Wirf ihn!

OFFICER 3: Jetzt! Jetzt!

OFFICER 1: Nun, Hans—(JACK *pulls him off balance*)

ALL OFFICERS: Bravo!

OFFICER 2: **Der shafts immer!**

OFFICER 4: (*to* WAITER) Herr Ober, Bier für uns alle!

JACK: No, Hands—(*Drawing them away*) Bess leave us darkies get quainted . . . you know, chomp a few bananas an all—

OFFICERS 3 *and* 4: (*laughing*) Er muss eine Banane essen! Ja!

OFFICER 2: He pleases you, the new Kamerad, Herr Boxer!

JACK: (*drawing them further*) Man, Ah'm happy as a cow with six tits. (*Shrieks of laughter.* THEY *go.* JACK *waves after them*) Weenersane! Donker! (*Returning*) **Wish they'd start a war up and keep them boys busy.**

NEGRO: (*standing at table*) You forgiff I am employed in siss, please.

JACK: Thass awright, chief. Needed some ex'cise anyway.

NEGRO: I am nutt chiff. I am son from ser chiff.

JACK: Oh, yeah? Well, take a pew here with the fiel'-nigger's boy. (THEY *sit,* JACK *pours*)

NEGRO: You are ser Boxer, ja?

JACK: Thass me. When Ah workin at it.

NEGRO: From Amerika kommen.

JACK: Yeah, kommen and goin. You never been there, Ah guess.

NEGRO: Nein. I haff nutt zere ser purpose. Iss gutt?

JACK: Sometimes. Ain been there a while myself.

NEGRO: You learn zere gutt make ser laughink.

JACK: Oh, thanks.

NEGRO: Please, iss nutt uffenz. Must I learn also, I sink.

JACK: (*laughs*) Seem like you leff it kina late.

NEGRO: Iss better, nein?

JACK: Yeah, mebbe so . . . Well, here's to us fish outa water.

 (THEY *drink*)

NEGRO: Away much long iss to hurt now. You.

JACK: Might say that.

NEGRO: I am feeling. I haff in Europe sree year so.

JACK: Lawd. Lit out for good, huh?

NEGRO: Please?

JACK: Vamoose fum de ole country, Africa.

NEGRO: Ah! You sink I go for nutt be zere, nein, nein. I go so I
 komm zere back.

JACK: How zat?

NEGRO: Mit more knowings.

JACK: Oh! Ah gotcha.

NEGRO: Student.

JACK: Yeah. Nevah touch it myself.

NEGRO: I do nutt tell to giff shame inn.

JACK: Huh? No, Ah'm with you, man. What all you studyin?

NEGRO: Ser Law and ser Finanz and ser Chemikals-mining.

JACK: My, my, my.

NEGRO: Ja, makes ser headache!

(JACK *laughs with him*)

JACK: **Better go warn de chief bout dis one!**

NEGRO: Please? You haff choke mit ser fazzer?

JACK: Naw . . . But Ah thought Mistah White running things down there.

NEGRO: Now, ja.

JACK: They gonna letya help, huh?

NEGRO: So, I vatch.

JACK: They ain leavin go, man. No place.

NEGRO: Zumorrow, nein.

JACK: Nex Wensdy nine neither.

NEGRO: Sey make here ser war soon, ja?

JACK: So?

NEGRO: Iss like drunken peoples, Sree mann, fife mann, hitting one ozzer—you haff see, Boxer! All ser teess mit bloot, out-spitten! **Up all ser eatings, POUAH, POUAH!** Sey make so enough ser war, plack mann fly out from ser mouss. I sink.

JACK: (*takes it in, then lifts his glass*) Here's to you an me an de "How Long Blues."

NEGRO: Please?

JACK: Drink up.

NEGRO: Ah, Boxer. Goes like you Pessimismus in Amerika all plack mann, I am fearing.

JACK: Well, don't go by me, buddy.

NEGRO: Ach, aber ja. Goes plack Champion so, goes kleine plack mann so! **Logik, nein?**

JACK: **He a bitch, ain he.**

NEGRO: Bad, stronk peoples to be so.

JACK: Oh, man, we strong on cryin there, thassall.

NEGRO: Nein, was slafe. Slafe nutt stronk, he die. Cry iss from ser life inn.

JACK: Well, it sure the wrong kina strong to git leff with when you ain slavin no more.

NEGRO: You komm gutt out. You.

JACK: Outa where.

NEGRO: Ser slafe. I see.

JACK: Ah dunno. Juss went the whole hog, man.

NEGRO: Please?

JACK: Shoot it all. You know: jump.

NEGRO: Ja, exakt. (*Points at him*) Ser bekinnink-man.

JACK: Naw, Ah ain tried ta start nothin. (NEGRO *bursts out laughing*) **What so funny bout dat?**

NEGRO: (*rocking with laughter*) Oh, Boxer, Boxer, Boxer, ven I am to chumping in Afrika, I hope so much nossing vill I make!

(GOLDIE *bursts in*)

GOLDIE: Jack! All over town I—oh, you busy?

(NEGRO *rises*)

JACK: Don' run off, man—

GOLDIE: Gotta talk to ya, Jack.

NEGRO: So, I go. (JACK *rises.* NEGRO *removes object from shirt*) Please, you take?

JACK: Oh, hey,—

NEGRO: Please. My fazzer giff.

JACK: (*hesitates, then takes it*) Wish you all the luck in the worl, man, thanks.

NEGRO: Also you. You keep mit, ja?

JACK: Sure. Zat what it's for? Luck?

NEGRO: Nein. For hurt from spirits.

JACK: Yeah.

NEGRO: Gootbye, Boxer. (NEGRO *bows and goes*)

JACK: OK, I'm listenin.

GOLDIE: Well . . . we got a match.

JACK: How much Ah get for losin it?

GOLDIE: Huh?

JACK: Yeah, Ah'm listenin.

GOLDIE: **How the hell does he know!**

JACK: Mah witch-doctor tole me.

GOLDIE: Look! Lemme first explain what Smitty—

JACK: Boss, Ah know whut Smitty. They askin fo a straight fight, they ain't sendin Smitty—

GOLDIE: Whattaya gettin sore, the guy calls me up—

JACK: Nobody sore. How much it worth?

GOLDIE: Fred's got this kid, see—

JACK: Now, boss, you ain't hearin good.

GOLDIE: Eighty-twenty split. A hundred G's guarantee.

JACK: Mm, boy! **Pretty nice fo plain ole layin down, huh!**

GOLDIE: And they'll cut the rap to six months for ya.

JACK: Well! **See all folks kin do when evvybody pitch in?**

GOLDIE: Jackie, I don't blame you for—

JACK: Any special roun they like me to dive in?

GOLDIE: He says we can work all that out.

JACK: Uh huh. An whut you say?

GOLDIE: I said it stinks but I'll let him know later.

JACK: (*pointing to champagne*) Right. Sen him a bottle a this, an tell him suck it through a straw.

GOLDIE: No thinkin it over.

JACK: How long you my manager?

GOLDIE: Five-six years.

JACK: Then why you gotta ask?

GOLDIE: Why? Cause I gotta eat, that's why! What am I managin here, for God's sake! What else you got in fronta you—

JACK: Don't try an sell me, boss.

GOLDIE: Big shot! Send him champagne! On what? The fights you have with your girl, maybe? **On a ten percent like this my enemies should live!**

JACK: Ah know it, man. Time to fine fresh meat.

GOLDIE: Well, what the hell you need me for, anyway!

act 2 / scene five   127

JACK: Yeah, been thinkin bout that—

(*The* FOUR OFFICERS *charge in.* THEY *carry a rope*)

OFFICER 4: (*to* WAITER) Herr Ober, Bier für uns alle!

GOLDIE: Jack, let's go talk to him, they're gonna keep after you, you're getting sick here—

JACK: No, you call it right—

OFFICER 1: (*giving* JACK *one end*) We make now to pull, Boxer?

JACK: Yeah, why not—

GOLDIE: Listen—

OFFICER 3: (*as* OFFICERS *take other end*) Erst, Hans!

JACK: There's no hard feelins, boss—

OFFICER 4: (*as* THEY *all line up*) **Nun gewinnen wir!**

GOLDIE: Jack—

JACK: Take all you need to get home on—

OFFICER 1: Prepared, mein herr?

JACK: (*getting a grip*) Anytime! (*Tug of war:* JACK *holds*)

GOLDIE: Oh, Jackie, oh, look at what you're doin—

JACK: (*giving ground*) It . . . ain't . . . good . . . but . . . it's . . . the . . . bess . . . Ah . . . can . . .

OFFICERS: (*pulling him out as* LIGHTS FADE) Ho-ya! Ho-ya! Ho-ya! Ho-ya!

(BLACKOUT. *Cymbal crash, followed by a tinny rendering of "Chiri-biri-bin" as* LIGHTS UP *on—*)

---

scene six

Cabaret Ragosy, Budapest

Small stage of a cabaret, audience unseen. A JUGGLER *in tights, working in time to the waltz, is finishing his turn.* LOUD APPLAUSE *as* HE *takes his bow;* RAGOSY, *now in evening dress and beaming, joins him on the stage and boosts the applause. Exit the* JUGGLER. RAGOSY *holds up his hand for silence.*

RAGOSY: És most, Hölgyeim es Uraim, amire mindanyian vártak! Bemutatom a Rágosy Kabaré föattrakcióját, Amerikai klasszikust "Uncle Thomas Kunyhóját." (*The saxophone begins playing "My Old Kentucky Home," and the* LIGHTING *becomes very roseate, as* TWO STAGEHANDS *position a papier-mâché weeping willow and a patch of grass.* RAGOSY *continues accordingly, describing the scene*) A jelenet a Mississippi . . . partjan jatszodik le . . . sek sek . . . Uncle Thomas és a little Éva élvezték a napkeltét . . . (*Winding up to bring them on*) Tehát bemutatjuk a világbajnokot Jack Jeffersont, elbübölö feleségével és néger barátjával!

(*Spatter of applause.* ELLIE *comes on as Little Eva, golden curls, etc.* JACK *follows her as Uncle Tom, shabby, gray wig, etc.* SHE *sits under "tree"*)

act 2 / scene six   129

ELLIE: Here, Uncle Tom, do come and sit beside me.

JACK: Deed Ah will, Miss Eva. On dis lubly ole grassy bank.

ELLIE: See how beautiful the clouds are, Tom. And the water too.

JACK: An you right widdem, Miss Eva, you de byootifluss of all.

ELLIE: But, friend, why do you seem sad this evening?

JACK: Oh, Miss Eva, you and de Massah so kine ter Ole Tom he juss gotta cry bout it now and den.

ELLIE: Yes. We are happy here.

JACK: It like a plantation fum de Good Book, yessum. You de brightest lil sperrit Ah evah seed, Miss Eva.

ELLIE: Oh, Tom, sing about the Spirits Bright, would you?

JACK: Juss gittin set to. (*Piano gives him a chord and accompanies. Sings.*)

Ah sees a ban uh Sperrits Bright
Dat tase de glo-ries dere—

(*Mock* GROAN *from the audience*)

Dey are all robed in spotliss white
An wavin palm dey bear.
Ef Ah had wings—

(*Another mock* GROAN, *a* TITTER, *a* VOICE *saying "következö";* JACK *stops, the piano stops. A moment of uncertainty*)

ELLIE: Oh, but look who has come to make us lively, Tom!

(*Enter* TICK *as Topsy, grinning and prancing*)

TICK: Hee, hee, hee!

ELLIE: Dear me, Topsy, why do you behave so!

TICK: Speck cause Ah jes plain ole wicked, Miss Eva!

JACK: What dis lil black imp done now?

TICK: Hee, hee, hee!

ELLIE: How old are you, Topsy?

TICK: Ah dunno, missy.

ELLIE: Don't you know how old you are? Who was your mother?

TICK: Ah dunno, missy. Nevah had no mother.

ELLIE: What do you mean? Where were you born?

TICK: Ah dunno, missy. Nevah wuz bo'n.

ELLIE: But Topsy, think a moment. Someone must have made you!

TICK: Nobody's Ah knows on, missy. Ah specks Ah jes growed!

ELLIE: Oh, Topsy—

TICK: Hee, hee, hee!

JACK: Awright, you shifless heathen, give us a breakdown an git back to yo stinks—

(*Piano and drums, assisted by* ELLIE, *who produces a tambourine, and* JACK, *a Jew's harp.* TICK *sings*)

TICK:
I always think I'm up in Heaven
When I'm down in Dixieland,
I've got an angel of a Mammy,
Out in Alabamy,
Of the good old fashioned brand;
She taught me that it's wrong,
To stay up all night long;
Go to sleep my baby,
That's Mammy's little fav'rite song.

(*Dances through the next chorus,* JACK *joining him,* ELLIE *continuing on the tambourine. The audience seems to like this better, but as* TICK, *breathless, resumes singing, they again grow more and more restless*)

Everybody loves somebody
Down in dear old Dixieland,
The pretty flowers in the garden,
Keep their heads a noddin,
When you walk by hand in hand;
The gals down there are very plain—

(RAGOSY *tries to quiet audience*)

And every other lane's a lovers lane,
That's why—*

(RAGOSY *pulls* TICK *from the stage, motioning to* JACK *and* ELLIE *to continue.* ELLIE *reclines in a moribund attitude against the tree as the saxophone commences with "Old Black Joe"*)

JACK: Is you feelin . . . weakish agin, Miss Eva?

ELLIE: Yes. There is something I must tell you, Uncle Tom.

(*Protest from the audience*)

JACK: It cain't be, Miss Eva, not yit—

ELLIE: Do not be gloomy! Look, those clouds, they are like great gates of pearl now.

(*More protests*)

JACK: No, Miss Eva, no—

ELLIE: And I can see beyond them . . . far, far off . . .

VOICE: Gyorsan, gyorsan!

JACK: (*kneeling*) Oh, Ah knows we cain't speck ta keep ya here wid us—

VOICE: Milyen unalmas!

ELLIE: Yes, I am going to a better country—

VOICE: A következö! (*Laugh*)

ELLIE: And I am going there before long, Uncle Tom . . . (*Groan*)

VOICES: Rémes! Rettentes!

JACK: Well, ef de Lawd needya back, Miss Eva—

VOICE: Hozd vissza a néger barátodat—!

JACK: Ah be hunkydory here—

VOICES: Rémes! Rémes!

(*A slow* HANDCLAP *starts in the audience, quickly building up with* FOOT-STAMPING *and* BOTTLE-KNOCKING)

ELLIE: Oh, dear Tom . . . take a tress of my . . .

VOICES: Borzasztó! Nevetséges!

(JACK *rises slowly, looks out at them*)

ELLIE: Take a tress of my golden hair . . . to . . . to . . . (SHE *stops as the* NOISE *gets louder.* RAGOSY *appears at the side of the stage, trying to quiet them again, but they grow more angry at this*)

VOICES:
Takaradjanak el!
Takaradjanak el!
Fogják meg!

(RAGOSY *tries to speak but cannot be heard;* ELLIE *runs from the stage.* JACK *pulls the Uncle Tom wig off and stands immobile, expressionless.* RAGOSY, *frightened, signals desperately—for* JACK *to get offstage, for the saxophonist to stop playing, for the electrician to cut the lights . . . the saxophone desists, and after a few attempts the electrician seems to find the right switch . . . as the* LIGHTS DIM OUT *on* JACK *the* NOISE *reaches a crescendo, then is cut off sharply in the* BLACKOUT *as, suddenly, at the extreme opposite end of the real stage,* MRS. BACHMAN *appears, white, pained, and haggard.* SHE *looks around at the real audience, then speaks*)

MRS. BACHMAN: I know what most of you watching this believe in, or think you believe in, or try to believe in. But I know something else too, I know what Black means, and not just to me because of my daughter, to everyone in here. All of us know, though it might take some of you a daughter you've cared for to make you say it, what it means, yes, means, what it is to you truthfully—BLACKNESS!—there, feel it, what it sets off in your heart, in the memories and words and shapes you think with, the dark to be afraid of, pitch black, black as dirt, the black hole and the black pit, what's burned or stained or cursed or hideous, poison and spite and the waste from your body and the horrors crawling up into your mind—I hate what I'm saying! As much as you do! I hate that it's so, I wish to God it weren't! And if it was God who intended it so, and still willed that color on a race of human beings, and brought us face to face here, how He must hate all of us! Go on imagining that time and justice can change it in you now, or that when it disappears in the singing of songs it's being destroyed. Tell yourselves it's only one more wrong to be righted, and that I'm a half-mad woman, oh, making far too much of it. Wait until it is your every other thought, like it is theirs, like it is mine. Wait until it touches your own flesh and blood.

(*As* SHE *slowly walks off, the* LIGHTS *on her fading, a distant* RUMBLE *of artillery fire is heard, which continues throughout the next scene—*)

---

scene seven

Railway station, Belgrade.

JACK *and* ELLIE *standing bedraggled in wet raincoats. Suitcases. Pools of light. Station empty.*

TICK: (*entering*) Nothin, man. Maybe one pullin out tonight.

JACK: Anybody know whut goin on dere?

TICK: Porter say dey just practicin.

JACK: Yeah.

ELLIE: What will we do, Jack?

JACK: I dunno yet.

ELLIE: Do you think we should—

JACK: Ah said Ah dunno yet!

ELLIE: All right, I heard you.

JACK: Play cards or somethin wid her, willya?

SMITTY: (*offstage*) Jack! (*Entering from a distance, catching his breath*) God, I'm glad I caught you . . .

JACK: Lay offa me, man.

SMITTY: It's sort of an emergency, Jack . . . back home. (*Takes out telegram*) Your mother's very low.

JACK: (*snatching it from him*) Gimme dat. (*Reads it. Holds onto it throughout scene*)

SMITTY: I'm sorry about this, feller.

JACK: Yeah. Thanks.

SMITTY: Maybe we could work something out for you, Jack. To go straight over now and then do the rest of it. I know you want to be there. (*Pause*) You might just make it, Jack. I've hired a car and I fixed up your passage from—

JACK: (*to himself*) Button comin loose here.

ELLIE: Yes? (*Pause*)

SMITTY: Christ, deal or no deal, it's worth a try, isn't it? Even just to let her feel you're on your way, she'd be—

JACK: Thanks for comin roun, man.

SMITTY: You can't stay over here now, anyway. Jack! It's finished here. You know that. Where do you go?

JACK: Don' wan none today, man.

SMITTY: All right, don't get sore—**I really thought—**

JACK: Ah seeya sometime. (*Pause*)

SMITTY: OK . . . (*Turns to go, stops*) What the hell is it for, though, all this. I mean, you're not a Boy Scout. What the hell is it, Jack. Keeping the belt a little bit longer? Staying champ a little while longer? I can't make you out.

JACK: Champ don' mean piss-all ta me, man. Ah bin it, all dat champ jive bin beat clear outa me. Dat belt a yours juss hardware, woulden even hole mah pants up. But Ah'm stuck widdit, see, a hunk of junky hardware, but it don' let go, it turnin green on me, but it still ain lettin go, Ah'm stuck as bad widdit as you all stuck wid needin it offa me—shake it loose, man! Knock me fo ten and take it, understan? Ah be much oblige!

SMITTY: Look, you know we'd rather have it straight—

JACK: Oh, ya would, huh.

SMITTY: Sure, and, Jack, if you weren't so damned good—

JACK: (*grabbing him*) Hunnerd million people ovah dere, ain'tya?

SMITTY: Yes, but—

JACK: Picked out de bess Hope ya got dere, ain'tya—?

TICK: Jack—

JACK: Ah wants a match widdim—

SMITTY: It's our way or nothing, feller—

JACK: Ah said a match widdim! An if you don' wanna gimme one, Ah gonna makeya, same's Ah done before, see—(*Releasing him*) **Ah gonna make em!** Gonna take mah funky suitcase an mah three-four hundred dollahs, an git mahself ta Mexico, howya like dat, man, right up nex ta ya, **gonna sit on dat line dere an wave you crummy belt atya an sing out Here Ah is**—

SMITTY: It's not going to work, Jack—

JACK: Dassall Ah got worth tryin now—(*Crumpling the telegram*) dis ain't, dis ain't, Ah know dis pass trying, Ah—

TICK: Easy—

ELLIE: Jack, I'm so sorry—

JACK: Took too much outa her, Ah guess, she musta—musta juss—(*Strikes himself a blow on the forehead, staggers*)

ELLIE: Oh, Jack—

JACK: Leave me lone.

CURTAIN ACT TWO

ACT 3

scene one

A street, Chicago.

In the BLACKOUT, *at slow tempo, approaching from the distance, "How Long Blues": bass drum, clarinet, trombone. As the* LIGHTS COME UP, NEGROES *are quietly filling the stage;* THEY *arrange themselves as if lining both sides of a street. A few* POLICEMEN *station themselves among them, and a group of* PRESSMEN *is deployed at one side. The* FUNERAL PROCESSION *appears, the* BANDSMEN *first, followed by the coffin—*GOLDIE *conspicuous as a pallbearer—behind it* CLARA, *supported by* SISTER, *then the* PASTOR. *The* MUSIC *stops as the coffin is set down. The* NEGROES *close in around it and the* PASTOR *addresses them.*

PASTOR: "When thou passes through de waters Ah will be wid thee, and de rivers, dey shall not overflow thee, fo Ah am de Lawd thy God, de Holyone of Isrel."

CONGREGATION: Amen.

PASTOR: Mosta you ain present today outa respeck to Sistah Tiny here, you-all here to stan up fo son Jack. An dass fine! He got a place in you heart, de Lawd muss wan him havin it. But Bredren, make a place dere fo dis humble woman, his momma, too. Take Sistah in you heart an let her show you somethin,

139

Bredren, Ah know you done took in what Jack bin showin you, but dis leass as good an mebbe worth more, praise de Lawd.

CONGREGATION: Amen.

PASTOR: "When thou passes through de waters Ah will be wid thee." Dis woman pass through dem all de days of her life. Born slave, like lotsa you poppas and mommas. Passed through dem waters. Passed through plain hungry waters, mean waters, cesspool-y waters. Currents like to swamp you—

CONGREGATION: Lawd!

PASTOR: Waters wid blood in em! Even passed through de waters of dat killer flood down Galveston, passin through one waters inter de nex one—

CONGREGATION: Lawd!

PASTOR: Sweatin in dem waters fum "cain't see" in de mornin till "cain't see" at night, an inter de nex one—

CONGREGATION: Jesus!

PASTOR: An when she coulden sweat no mo, passed through em juss shiverin an achin an sick—but whut wuz going long wid her!

CONGREGATION: Mah Savior!

PASTOR: Tell me dat!

CONGREGATION: Glory comin!

PASTOR: Amen! De Lawd say Ah'll be wid thee, de Lawd was passin through dem waters wid her, inter de nex one an de nex one and de nex, holdin her afloatin an liftin up de joy in her—

CONGREGATION: Hallelujah!

PASTOR: DASS whut she had, Bredren! Dass whut she show you! She din cuss dem waters—

CONGREGATION: No, Lawd!

PASTOR: She know whut evvybody know in deir heart here, **dere's ALWAYS dem waters, dere ALWAYS tribberlation, de nex one an de nex an we ALWAYS passin through—**

CONGREGATION: Can't hurt me!

PASTOR: **Ah is, an you is, an you chillun gonna, an anybody's chillun till kingdom come—**

CONGREGATION: Oh, yeah!

PASTOR: She din blame de Lawd fo not partin dem waters like de ole Red Sea! She knowed He done said, "Dey shall not overflow thee," an she TRUSTED her Lawd.

CONGREGATION: Jesus!

PASTOR: She knowed dat fifty year ago when we wuz nigh to GITTIN overflowed He give us a Moses an He did part dat sea an He took us outa bondage!

CONGREGATION: Hallelujah!

PASTOR: She knowed all de time she pine for her boy dat de Lawd workin in His own way—(CLARA *begins sobbing*) dat He ain't juss on tap evvy time we give a holler—

CONGREGATION: Oh my!

PASTOR: She felt de Lawd takin her fore she got ta see him, but she held on tight to dat—

(*Flurry of movement, photo-flashes, jostling*)

NEGRO 1: Whut gawn on dere—

PHOTOGRAPHER 1: This way, miss—

PHOTOGRAPHER 2: Excuse me—

GOLDIE: Say, can't you guys—

CLARA: (*going for* PHOTOGRAPHER 1) Gimme dat, you mother—

PASTOR: Sistah—

NEGRO 2: Who dat—

GOLDIE: (*checking* HER) For Godsakes—

POLICEMAN 1: No shoving there—

PASTOR: Gennulmen—

CLARA: Leggo me—

GOLDIE: Ignore em, just—

CLARA: You too, ya dirty pinkface pimp—

PASTOR: Sistah, dis ain no time—

CLARA: (*breaking away*) Yeah, oh yeah dis de time awright! Whut he doin here, whut any of em doin here—

SISTER: Clara—

CLARA: Look at em! **Howya feelin now, folks! All dress up dere watchin de fewnral? Ain'tya bought some flowahs?**

GOLDIE: (*to* PASTOR) I'm sorry about this—

CLARA: Sho you is! You an dat white bitch an de whole pack a ya—come on ovah to de box here, sugah, see how good y'all nail de lid down—

PASTOR: Sistah—

CLARA: No! Ah seed mah Momma Tiny's heart gittin busted, Ah seed her layin dere pinin and sick till she nothin but bone, Ah heard her beggin fo Jack—Who set him runnin! Who put de mark on him! Why she die so bad! Where all her trouble fum! Dem, dem, dem, dem, an Ah wanna make juss one of em —(*Goes for the audience*)

PASTOR: Sistah—(*Struggle*)

POLICEMAN 1: (*to* PASTOR) Look, if you can't handle em—

PASTOR: Bredren—

NEGRO 2: No, let her, man—

CLARA: **Ah gonna settle wid—**

SISTER: (*slaps* CLARA'S *face*) Behave yourself!

CLARA: (*falling on the coffin*) Oh help me, Momma Tiny, Ah wanna do right by ya, Don' leave me, Momma, Momma, Ah be good, please . . .

PASTOR: Oh, brudders and sistahs! Look out when Satan start a-lightin dat hate fire! Member who de Lawd say vingeance belong ta, member he fogit not de cry a de oppressed—

SCIPIO: (*concealed in the* CROWD) Dass right, chillun, suffer nice an easy—school em on it, boss!

PASTOR: Who talkin dere!

SCIPIO: (*appearing*) Me—ya no-name brudder!

PASTOR: Take dat off your head here—

SCIPIO: No! Went inta buy me a hat once, boss, Man say cover you head wid a hankie and DEN try it on—

PASTOR: Shame on you!

SCIPIO: Yeah, now you sayin it—shame on me, an shame on alla us, for BEIN de oppressed, an bein it, an bein it! Shame on us moanin low two hunnerd years here! Fo needin a big White Moses fo a daddy!

NEGRO 3: Amen, brudder!

PASTOR: Whut—

SCIPIO: Yeah! Shame on evvy Goodie-Book thumper like you! White man keep pullin de teeth outa you head an preacher here giving you de laughin-gas—

PASTOR: Ah warnin you, heathen—

SCIPIO: Ah warnin evvybody! **Warnin dat white gal an warnin dem po-lice ain nothin lass foever!**

NEGRO 2: Tell em!

SCIPIO: **Warnin dat dead woman Jesus wuzn't swimmin! Warnin mah people dat boy juss a shadow an dey livin black men whut gotta live long—**

NEGRO 3: Right!

SCIPIO: Don' Amen me! Makin believe you de Chillun of Isrel, fiery-furnacin an roll-on-Jordanin—you ain no Isrel! Dere— (*Points to* GOLDIE) *Dass* a Jew-man—see whut ya see! Look in de mirrah once an see whut ya see! Ah said de MIRRAH, not a lotta blue eyes you *usin* fo a mirrah, an hatin whut dey hates, de hair you got, de nose you got, de mouth you got, de—

PASTOR: Offissah, Ah'm askin you—

POLICEMAN 1: Right—

NEGRO 3: Whut dey doin—

SCIPIO: Hate dat woolly head, you gotta hate de man whut got it, brudders, dat man YOU—

POLICEMAN 2: (*to* SCIPIO) Move—

SCIPIO: Don' hate it, brudders—

NEGRO 5: Lemme through—

NEGRO 6: Stop em—

SCIPIO: (*as* POLICE *haul at him*) Champeen in your heart, but dey ain one a you—

NEGRO 4: Help him—

NEGRO 6: Dey hurtin him—

NEGRO 7: Quick—

NEGRO 8: Dey gonna kill him—

NEGRO 4: Let em have it—

POLICEMAN 3: Move—

PASTOR: Bredren—

NEGRO 1: (*holdin back* CLARA) Sistah—

NEGRO 5: No cuttin—

NEGRO WOMAN 1: Help—

NEGRO 8: Cut em—

POLICEMAN 3: There—

NEGRO 4: Gimme dat—

POLICEMAN 1: Come on, call em out—!

(POLICE WHISTLES *above the pandemonium; flashing night-sticks and swinging fists; the coffin is hurried off;* LIGHTS BEGIN FADING *and* HOOFBEATS *are heard, then* SCREAMS)

NEGRO VOICES:
Look out—
No, dis way—
Brudders—
Pull em off—
No—
You mother—
Here—
Lemme git one—
Move—
Teddy—

Run—
Here—
Mah head, mah head, mah head, mah head—

(DARKNESS. *Silence.* LIGHTS UP *on*—)

---

scene two

Pop Weaver's office, New York.

CAP'N DAN *and* SMITTY, *followed in by* POP *and* FRED. *Newspapers.*

CAP'N DAN: Look at this, look at this—**I can't even think straight**—

SMITTY: I told you, he's out for—

CAP'N DAN: Don't tell me again! One more lousy picture of him and that belt. One more newsie sneakin down there to see him—

FRED: What about the ones on me up here, Dan'l?

CAP'N DAN: Say you can't promote it! Say he's askin too much!

FRED: After that piece in the *Journal?*

SMITTY: Here.

FRED: **Will Fight Kid for Carfare and a Watermelon.**

CAP'N DAN: Christ—

POP: Maybe we could pay him off to retire, Dan—

CAP'N DAN: **Twenty years, what I'd give for twenty years—**

POP: He wouldn't need to lay down, we'd get the belt back—

CAP'N DAN: Sure, and have a coon champ retire undefeated!

SMITTY: What if we promise him a straight fight later on if he dives on this one.

FRED: Later on.

SMITTY: You know.

CAP'N DAN: He's too goddam smart for that!

FRED: Just an idea now, but supposing we sign it, then something gets put on his sponge, or in his water . . .

SMITTY: It's worked before, Dan.

POP: I would hate to hang this on something from a drugstore.

CAP'N DAN: Jesus, listen to us, **look what that boogie's got us down to here—**

POP: Don't excite yourself, Dan—

CAP'N DAN: On the verge, I tell them! You know what I look like, stalling for months and making excuses, and all he winds up is smack on the border like a boil on the whole country's ass?

FRED: All right! Then why don't we sign it and have it, for chrissake! He'll never be in shape the way he was in Reno—

CAP'N DAN: Get it in writing—

FRED: Here, look at the gut on him—And look at that Kid—

POP: Fred—

FRED: Honest to God, he's better, every time out, listen, four KO's and three decisions since April, and I've got him with Brady now, we're giving him all kinds of angles on the nigger, like how when he smiles—

CAP'N DAN: **Do I have to hear this?**

FRED: Wait, no, I mean it—when you're doin a smile, see, your mouth's kina open and your teeth's not clenched, so you hit him when he's smilin, you can bust a guy's jaw—**That's no bull, that's from an osteopath!**

CAP'N DAN: Pop, you try, go down there yourself—

POP: Dan, I don't discourage very easy, but I'm afraid there's only one safe bet for us. It isn't ideal—

CAP'N DAN: Come on, come on—

POP: Even if he's still as good as he was, Dan, the man is no spring chicken any more. And you know what happens. Maybe not by tomorrow, or the next day either, but it will happen, Dan. The legs'll start to go, like everybody else's—**it's all downhill.**

CAP'N DAN: Two years? Three years?

POP: Whenever he's ripe we throw him in with Fred's boy—

CAP'N DAN: Pop, can't you help me?

POP: Taking this on was a real mistake, Dan. I'd like to follow through but that's the best we have.

FRED: I'd go along—

SMITTY: We could say we're waiting on account of the war—

FRED: **We could give a big play to the middleweights—**

CAP'N DAN: Pop—Jesus!

POP: We can work it, let's put it on ice—

CAP'N DAN: There ain't that much ice in this whole rotten world—

FRED: What do we do then—kill him? (*Pause*)

CAP'N DAN: How broke is he, Smitty?

SMITTY: They live in a flophouse and he trains in a barn.

CAP'N DAN: Any dough from outside?

SMITTY: Friends, a little.

CAP'N DAN: Find out who, we'll stop it—anybody sparring with him?

POP: Dan, what's the point—

SMITTY: A couple of rubes from Texas—

CAP'N DAN: Pull them out, send them home. No exhibitions, nothing, no contact, cut him off—

POP: He's not going to give, Dan—

CAP'N DAN: He made the last move he had and now we'll screw him with it, now we're gonna show him what a bad move it was, this time we ain't askin, or offerin, or tryin, or pussyfootin round this like a bunch of pansies, we got him so close we can reach out and squeeze—**we're gonna squeeze that dinge so goddam hard soon a fix is gonna look like a hayride to him!**

POP: Dan, don't get him any madder than he is—

CAP'N DAN: Start scouting out a place we can hold it—

POP: We're making us two mistakes in a row, Dan—

CAP'N DAN: Havana, maybe, the bigger the better—

POP: I mean it. Tell your people we just can't deliver.

CAP'N DAN: No, I tell them we might need a hand—

FRED: Say, wait—

CAP'N DAN: You get busy, talk to Goldie—I want all that set!

POP: We're way out over our head now, you know.

CAP'N DAN: So is he, friend. Let's see who goes under.

(BLACKOUT. *Enter* CLARA *in* SPOTLIGHT, *as distant* BELL *slowly chimes midnight.* SHE *clutches a flimsy stained garment to her*)

CLARA: **Do it, soon, soon, goin good now, drag him on down. Oh won'tya, fo me an mah momma an evvy black-ass woman he turn his back on, for evvy gal wid a man longside dreamin him a piece a what HE got, fo alla his let-down secon-bess sistahs, all Mistah Number One's lil ugly sistahs—ssh!—dey's moonin fo de day you does it, dey's some sleepin an plenny** itchin quiet, dey's me aholda dis, an we drawin him, drawin him. Oh, where dem rosy cheeks gonna hit him, don' never stop now, offa dat high horse an on down de whole long mud-track in fronna him, years gawnta nothin, feelin em, dere, limpin an slippin an shrinkin an creepin an sinkin right in— **Call him to ya, Momma!** (*Holds out the garment at full length: a nightgown, stiff with blood and excrement*) Soon, baby, soon.

(LIGHT *fades slowly into* BLACKOUT; *thudding of a punching-bag is heard;* LIGHTS UP *on—*)

---

scene three

A disused barn, Juarez.

By the light of a few kerosene lanterns, JACK *pounds at a punching-bag, which is steadied from behind by* PACO, *a Mexican boy.* TICK *claps his hands in time with him.*

TICK: Slow it up, slow it up—

JACK: Whut—?

TICK: Slow it, let dat sweat out—(*Claps at a slower tempo, sings*)

Times is very hard,
Gimme ten-cent worth a lard,
Gonna keep mah skillet greasy
If Ah can, can, can,
Gonna keep mah skillet—

(JACK *delivers a last impatient slam and turns away from it*)

Nuff?

JACK: Yeah, Ah'm pushin.

TICK: OK, Paco, dassit.

JACK: Six-thirty mañana.

PACO: Si, Campeón. We ron?

JACK: Yeah, we run.

PACO: I com for wek op?

JACK: No, Ah be up. (PACO *starts putting gear in order*)

TICK: (*leading* JACK *to a trestle table*) Wearin us out, baby, comin on fine . . . (JACK *sits,* TICK *pulls his gloves off*) Oughta raise de bag up higher tomorrer, startya liftin em, huh? (JACK *lies down*) Yeah . . . (*Working on him*) bout a foot or so. You know, seein how big dat Kid is . . . (JACK *does not reply*) Sho a funny size fo a Kid, ain he? **Soun like somethin gone wrong wid his glans!**

JACK: Don' try unwindin me, man. Juss rub.

TICK: Yassuh, shine em up—

JACK: (*to* PACO, *who has picked up his gloves*) Leave dose, willya.

PACO: Si, Campeón.

TICK: You cain work out tonight no mo, Ah mean—

JACK: How much dat guy say he giveya for em.

TICK: Oh.

JACK: Fifty?

(BARKING *is heard*)

TICK: You gloves, baby. (JACK *doesn't reply*)

PACO: (*looking out*) Viene la señorita.

JACK: Put em in a piece a paper she don' see em.

TICK: Well, you kin work wid de heavy ones, time bein. Bettah fo ya, anyhow.

(*More* BARKING. ELLIE *enters, carrying a dish with a napkin over it.* SHE *wears sunglasses*)

PACO: Buenas noches—

TICK: Mmm-MM! Whut dat old lanlady whip up tonight?

PACO: (*at the door shooing away the dogs*) Andale! Vaya!

ELLIE: I wish they would feed their dogs around here.

JACK: You feedin yours here, ain'tya.

TICK: (*resuming massage*) Set it down, hon—how mah gal today?

ELLIE: All right. You?

TICK: Fine! Shoulda seed him burn up dat road dis mornin, right fum de bridge to Pedrilla an up ta—

JACK: (*to* ELLIE, *not looking at her*) Gonna say it or whut.

ELLIE: No, nothing, Jack. No cables. Nothing.

JACK: Thanks.

TICK: Man, we be hearing pretty soon. Worry juss makin you tight, dass why ya ain sweatin like ya oughta—

JACK: Juss you rub, man.

TICK: Ass me, we's lucky dey ain sign it up yet! Givin us all dis good gittin-ready time?

ELLIE: Let him eat before it gets cold, Tick.

TICK: Yeah, switch you brain off a while an—

JACK: Leave it.

TICK: OK, OK. (*Long pause*)

ELLIE: Jack—

(TRAIN WHISTLE)

PACO: Tren from El Paso.

ELLIE: Yes?

TICK: Yeah . . . Whistle like dat crossin ovah.

PACO: Hasta mañana, señores.

TICK: So long, kid.

(PACO *goes*)

ELLIE: Why don't you come back and wash now, Jack. I'll wait here if you like.

JACK: Smelling pretty strong, huh?

ELLIE: You know that's not what I—

JACK: (*sitting up*) Dass inuff, man.

ELLIE: Jack, will you talk to me.

JACK: Tick gawn ovah on a erran, you kin go walk roun dere a lil widdim—

ELLIE: No, I want to talk to you—

JACK: Mebbe git a ice-cream soda, lookit some Mericans or somethin—

ELLIE: Jack—

TICK: Not wid me, boss—**Ah ain strollin wid no white gal in no Texas!** (*To* ELLIE, *as he goes out with the package*) Hole de fort, hon, won't be too long.

(*Pause.* TRAIN WHISTLE)

ELLIE: Let them go ahead, Jack.

JACK: Take dem specs off. Ah cain hardly see ya.

ELLIE: (*doing so*) I didn't think you wanted to.

JACK: You readin mah mine now?

ELLIE: Jack—

JACK: Ah toleya keep outa dis, din Ah.

ELLIE: I can't. Please, let them, you have to.

JACK: Finely battin fo de home team, huh.

ELLIE: Cable them tonight, please—

JACK: **Finely come roun to it**—

ELLIE: Jack, don't bitch me now—

JACK: Ah toleya—

ELLIE: No, I don't care! Forget what you told me! Say yes and get it over with, for God's sake! You're letting them do this to you, it's worse—

JACK: Worse fo you, mebbe—

ELLIE: Jack, it's slow poison here, there's nothing else to wait for, just more of it, you've had enough—please, you're being paralyzed—

JACK: Wid you mebbe—

ELLIE: All right, yes, with me too, with everything but hammering that stupid bag there! You're not your own man any more—

JACK: Now you rollin—

ELLIE: How can you be your own man, they have you! They do and you know it, you're theirs, at least you can buy yourself back from them—

JACK: **Sold—one-buck nigger fo de lady!**

ELLIE: Let it sound the way it is! Run when they push you and back when they pull you, work yourself sick in this hell-hole for nothing, and tell me you're not theirs—here, look at the grease you swallow for them, look at the bedbug bites on your arms, and the change in your pockets and the blotches in your eyes—

JACK: Don' leave de smell out—

ELLIE: The two of us smell! Whatever turns people into niggers —there—(*Shows her neck*) it's happening to both of us—

JACK: Wish comin true, huh—

ELLIE: No, never this, it wasn't this—

JACK: Sing it, sistah!

ELLIE: I want you there fighting them again, that's what I wish now, I want to watch when you're knocking them down for this, dozens of them, God help them, wipe it off on all of them—

JACK: How bout rooster-fightin, plenty right here—

ELLIE: Listen to me, please—

JACK: Oughta look inta dat—

ELLIE: You'd fight them and you'd be with your friends and you'd—

(JACK *crows like a rooster*)

JACK: **Somebody wanna sign me?**

ELLIE: Maybe we could live then, damn you!

JACK: Lil frame house, tree in front?

ELLIE: Anything!

JACK: Nice quiet street?

ELLIE: Anywhere! A place!

JACK: Lil cozy—

ELLIE: A kitchen!

JACK: Put de cat out? Tuck in de kids?

ELLIE: Oh, you're just hateful!

JACK: Well Ah gonna tellya whut de livin like, baby, far as Ah concern—

ELLIE: Get away from me—

JACK: Yeah, Ah put you straight on it—an alla you, too. Ah wen into a fair once and dere wuz dis old pug, see, give anybody two bucks who stan up a roun widdim—perfessional set-up, reggerlation ring an all, cep dey had rope juss on three sides, dass right, de back side wuz de tent. So Ah watches a couple git laid out real quick in dere, but he don' look dat red-hot ta me, see, so Ah climbs in widdim. An Ah doin awright fo a youngster, when all it once he bulls me up gainss dat tent-side a de ring an SLAM, WHAM, somebody behine dere conks me, right through de canvas, musta use a two by four, an evvy time Ah stans up he shove me back agin, an SLAM, dere's anudder, down she come—good story, huh?

ELLIE: Jack—

JACK: Dass how it go like Ah knows it, baby—

ELLIE: Sometimes, sometimes—

JACK: All de way now! dass where Ah is and dass whut Ah'm
gittin, gonna git it de same sayin Yassuh, Nossuh, don' mattah
whut Ah does—Ah in dere, unnerstan? An Ah don' wan you
watchin, or helpin, or waitin, or askin, or hannin me you jive
bout livin, or anythin fromya but OUT, Ah mean OUT—

ELLIE: What—

JACK: How goddamn plain Ah gotta make it for ya!

ELLIE: Jack—if you want other girls—

JACK: Git you stuff ready, train out ten o'clock.

ELLIE: No, no, I won't, no—

JACK: When Tick come Ah sen him ovah—

ELLIE: Jack—

JACK: Bettah start movin—

ELLIE: Stop it—

JACK: Ah pologize actin so yellah up ta—

ELLIE: Wait, you have to stop it—

JACK: All Ah has to is be black an die, lady—

ELLIE: I want to stay, even if we—

JACK: Stay wid you own, lady—

ELLIE: What are you doing!

JACK: Quit dat, quit it, short an sweet—

ELLIE: I won't go—

JACK: You knowed it comin, start movin—

ELLIE: Wait—

JACK: Don' cross me now—

ELLIE: Jack, I thought we'd save something, please—

JACK: Ah said MOVE—

ELLIE: Please, I only—

JACK: MOVE! You through widdit now—

ELLIE: Jack—

JACK: No mo lousy grub you gotta puke up, no more a ya lookin like a wash-out rag here, wid you eye twitchin alla—

ELLIE: Don't—I don't care—

JACK: Juss MOVE—

ELLIE: I'll take better—

JACK: Hangin on me, dead weight—

ELLIE: No, not for you—

JACK: Start—

ELLIE: Jack, I'll find a job, please—

JACK: Ah toleya when mah momma die, Ah toleya leave me be a while, now—

ELLIE: Jack, I can't run anymore, not by myself—

JACK: You got you people and you a—

ELLIE: No, listen—

JACK: You a young woman an you gonna—

ELLIE: Please, I'd never—

JACK: Gonna fine—

ELLIE: No one else, I'd—

JACK: Tough titty—

ELLIE: Just—

JACK: Move, or goddamn you—

ELLIE: Why can't you wait at least! Wait till you've given me a chance to make you happy—one chance, only one—**I swear I've never had one**—

JACK: Too big a order all aroun!

ELLIE: No, I won't go—

JACK: Wanna drag it out, huh—

ELLIE: I won't, I can't—

JACK: Den Ah gonna wise you up good now, you gray bitch—

ELLIE: You can't make me go, stop doing this—

JACK: Why you think Ah ain't put a han to yo fo how long, why ya think it turn me off juss lookin atya—

ELLIE: Stop it—

JACK: You stayin, stay fo it all. Ya know why? Does ya, honeybunch? Cause evvy time you pushes dat pinch-up face in fronna me, Ah sees where it done got me, dass whut Ah lookin at, where an how come an de Numbah One Who, right down de line, girl, an Ah mean YOU, an Ah don' wanna give you NOTHIN, unnerstan? Ah cut it off firss!

ELLIE: Oh, I despise you—

JACK: Right, like alla resta ya—

ELLIE: Oh, I'd like to smash you—

JACK: Me an evvy udder dumb nigger who'd letya! Now go home an hustle one up who don' know it yet, plenny for ya, score em up—**watch out, brudders!** Oughta hang a bell on so dey hear you comin.

ELLIE: You mean this?

JACK: Look in mah purple eyes. (*Pause*)

ELLIE: You win, daddy. (SHE *turns and goes. Pause.* JACK *takes a swig from the water-bottle, gargles, spits, then walks to the punching-bag and starts to jab at it. For a few moments* HE *does not notice the entrance of a slightly shabby but imposing-looking Mexican,* EL JEFE. *Then, sensing someone behind him,* JACK *stops*)

act 3 / scene three   163

EL JEFE: I lessen you mek beeg denuncio, Campeón. So I nut com een.

JACK: Who you, mistah?

EL JEFE: Ees nut meester, Campeón. I seet now, yes? (*Sits*)

JACK: Whut you want?

EL JEFE: (*taking out a bottle and offering it*) You like?

JACK: No, Ah'm in trainin.

EL JEFE: Pliz?

JACK: Trainin. On a fight.

EL JEFE: Si, es terrible . . . for Negro, for peon, for avery poor peoples, **fight from meenit we out from dee modder.**

JACK: Ah astya whut you want, man.

EL JEFE: I hear, Campeón. Salud. (*Drinks*)

JACK: Look, Ah ain made no trouble wid none a you.

EL JEFE: (*laughs a bit*) Where ees dee fadders, compadre.

JACK: De whut?

EL JEFE: Dee fadders. Dee weengs. Ees all high ovair flying like anjel, you think, no? **El hombre solo.**

JACK: Whut you after, man?

EL JEFE: Maybe you halp soon pobre black amigos. You show heem ees solo nut posible . . . Que vida, eh?

JACK: (*moving to the door*) Man, you juss playin wid me, Ah'm gonna—

EL JEFE: (*standing*) No, I filling to you beeg compassion, my fran. Dees Mejico my cowntry, I ongry here, I keel here, I am fugitivo lik you much times. Bot ulways to love. You cowntry you nut love her and she nut you, unly mak bad drims ich odder.

(A CAR *has been approaching and is heard braking*)

VOICE OUTSIDE: Han venido, Jefe.

EL JEFE: Déjanlos entrar.

(*Pause. Enter* DIXON, GOLDIE, *and a young* AGENT)

DIXON: Good evening.

EL JEFE: Señores.

GOLDIE: Hello, Jack.

JACK: Yeah. OK. Ah'm listenin.

GOLDIE: Well . . . (*To* DIXON) All right? (DIXON *impassive*) They're makin it easier, Jack. I mean it's . . . They threw in now suspended sentence.

JACK: Yeah.

GOLDIE: You fight in Havana, you hand yourself in, you go to court, one-two-three, and that's all.

JACK: Go on, boss.

GOLDIE: Well . . .

JACK: Don' be shy bout it.

GOLDIE: Jackie, it's quits now . . . (*Stops, pained*)

JACK: (*to* DIXON) Mebbe you tell me.

DIXON: Apart from your original conviction, Jefferson, which carries, you remember, up to three years, there are quite a few other violations, involving, for example: jumping bail, using the mails to bribe officials in Canada, tax irregularities, falsifying passports—

GOLDIE: They'll throw the whole book on you. Till God knows when.

JACK: Tell me de ress of it, mistah. You law up dere an Ah down here. Cain leave dat out—(*To* EL JEFE) Can he, man? You country, ain't it, man?

EL JEFE: (*downcast*) Si, compadre.

AGENT: It is perfectly legal, once we've ascertained where a wanted man is, to request cooperation of the parties in charge there.

EL JEFE: Perdóname, Campeón, We nid from dem, comprende? **We nut like. We nid,**

JACK: Yeah.

EL JEFE: Go Habana. Ees batter.

DIXON: I would think so.

GOLDIE: Yon finish inside there, what'll you have, Jack. **An old man he'll be.**

JACK: Well . . . Ah'm far long awready, boss. Ah'm stannin here gittin older evvy minnit. An Ah'm goin right through dat door—(*Moves*)

EL JEFE: No—(*Draws pistol*) compadre! (*Steps in front of* JACK)

JACK: Use it if ya got to, man.

EL JEFE: Hombre, ivin I lat you, where now you—

JACK: Dassall up to me, man. (*Advances*)

EL JEFE: I tie weeth rope, you do theess—!

JACK: Oh, Ah killya firss, man. (*Advances*)

EL JEFE: Hijo, averyplace catch on you, I swear you, all geev you to gringos, Huerta, Obregón—

JACK: (*advancing*) Ah goin out de door, man—

EL JEFE: Hombre . . . (*Clicks backhammer*) Hombre—

JACK: Gimme a break, fo Gawdsake.

EL JEFE: No! Who you halpeeng een your life, nadie, OSS now you halp—(JACK *advances*) Cabrón, wan more—

JACK: Well, mebbe it be doin me a favor. (*Steps around* EL JEFE, *keeps walking*)

GOLDIE: Jack—(EL JEFE *raises his pistol*)

DIXON: In the leg—

AGENT: Don't—

EL JEFE: Chíngate, gringo—(*Aims at* JACK'S *back, calls*) You stuppeeng? Hombre, nut stuppeeng, I—

(JACK *at the doorway, suddenly stops, then slowly moves backward as* TICK *and* TWO MEXICANS *enter.* THEY *carry in* ELLIE'S *mudsmeared and dripping body*)

MEXICAN: Se tiró en el pozo. Acabada.

EL JEFE: Díos.

JACK: Whut . . . whut . . . ?

TICK: Threw hersel down de . . .

JACK: No, no, Jesus—

TICK: **Down de well, Ah coulden—**

JACK: Git somebody, gimme de bottle—why she—

TICK: Busted her neck, man.

JACK: Honey! Honey, baby, please, sugar, no—! Whut Ah—whut Ah—whut Ah—baby, whut Ah done to ya, whut you done, honey, honey, whut dey done to us . . .

EL JEFE: (*turns away*) No puedo mirarlo.

GOLDIE: Jack. Jack. Anything I can . . . (JACK *nods*) Anything. What, Jack.

JACK: Set dat fuckin fight up! Set it up, set it up! **Ah take it now!**

(BLACKOUT. *Sound of* PRESSES *rolling.* CAP'N DAN *appears in* SPOTLIGHT: HE *smokes a cigar, wears a white carnation, carries a small valise, and is jubilant*)

CAP'N DAN; **Well, there's such a commotion on this you'd think we just organized the Second Coming! Tickets? They're going down without em, hey, honest to God, it does your heart good, songs about the Kid, pictures of the Kid stuck up in windows, stores, you pass a brick wall it has KID painted on it, people on the street saying Well, we got the Hope, Dan!— cost me two hundred in cigars already—and wait, wait, I bet you can't guess who's refereein—Brady! Oh, will they eat that up, when he's given the count and he's—what? No, he ain't in on it, neither is the Kid, who the hell wants that! But he's the one who lost it, and the whole world's gonna see him take it in his hand again, and hold it up and pass it on, like the Kid'll pass it—**(BOAT WHISTLE *interrupts him*) **OK! This time we'll keep it in the family!**

(DAN *exits*)

---

scene four

A street, somewhere in the United States.

As DAN *exits a group of* NEGROES *swarms on,* ONE *of them rapidly beating on a bass drum,* ANOTHER *holding up a torch in one hand and a pail in the other, a* THIRD *scribbling on a long sheet of foolscap; the* OTHERS *clamorously surround them, calling out their names and throwing money into the pail.* DRUMMING *throughout.*

NEGRO 1: Oscar Jones—

NEGRO 2: Pearl Whitney—

NEGRO 3: Jasper Smollett—

PAIL MAN: Write em down dere—throw in dem nickels—

NEGRO 4: Charlie Webb—

NEGRO 5: Bill Montgomery—

PAIL MAN: More! Who else here—**Sign on de telegram to Jack— fi' cents—**

NEGRO 4: Read out de message, man—

NEGRO 1: Let em all hear it!

PAIL MAN: **"HELLO JACK BESS NACHUL FIGHTER IN DE WORL—"** (CHEERS) **"HOME FOLKS PUNCHIN RIGHT WIDYA—SIGNED—"** (*The* CHEERING *drowns him, a* VOICE *over it sings—*)

VOICE: Hot boilin sun comin ovuh—

NEGRO 6: Waltuh Peters!

SEVERAL JOINING IN: Hot boilin sun comin ovuh—

NEGRO 2: **We show ya!**

MORE JOINING: Hot boilin sun comin ovuh—

NEGRO 7: **Ah'm on dere!**

ALL: (*singing*) AN HE AIN'T A-COMIN DOWN—

(*Whooping and cheering,* THEY *run off, the sound of their* VOICES *fading into the* ROAR *of the* CROWD *as* LIGHTS COME UP *on—*)

---

scene five

Oriente Racetrack, Havana.

Entrance gate. Two huge ornate wooden columns; suspended high between them, a banner featuring the simplified figures of a white boxer and a black one locked in combat. A cluster of ticketless WHITE MEN *at the barrier,* ALL *feverishly trying to follow the fight by the roars of the crowd and through* ONE *of their number perched high on a column. In the fierce heat all coats have been discarded, most shirts as well: heads are bound with handkerchiefs or covered with cheap straw hats—a few of these still left are hawked by a couple of ragged* CUBAN NEGRO BOYS.

MAN 1: (on column) No, Kid—block him—you're lettin him—

(ROAR)

MAN 2: Again?

MAN 3: Sounds like he—

MAN 1: No—but the dinge caught him right in the—Kid! Christ—

MAN 4: What—?

MAN 1: Don't back up—

MAN 6: (*through paper megaphone*) Use them arms already—

MAN 7: **Ten goddam rounds, ain't took a one yet—**

(ROAR, *as a* PINKERTON MAN *helps* MAN 8, a sunstroke victim, *through the gate*)

PINKERTON MAN 1: I toldya—leave the gate clear—

(ROAR)

MAN 1: Another one—

MAN 4: Just keep him off you—

(POP *appears at a side door.* MAN 8 doubles over, retching)

PINKERTON MAN 1: Move—**it's like an oven here—**

MAN 6: Time, for chrissake—

NEGRO BOY 1: (shaking a gourd in MAN 8's face) Eh! Eh! Eh! Eh!

MAN 1: Kid, quit clinchin—

MAN 8: Scram, ya dirty little—

MAN 1: BELL!

MAN 9: **Thank God!**

MAN 2: How the hell can he take it!

SMITTY: (*coming through a side door*) Jesus, Pop—

POP: You sure they got the high sign?

SMITTY: Two rounds ago!

POP: Then what—

SMITTY: Pop, I gave it four times, I know they got it, Goldie flicked the towel, Pop, we went over and over it—

MAN 4: (*to* MAN 1) How's it look—

MAN 1: He's collapsin there but so is the nigger—**puffin like a goddamn buffalo—**

MAN 2: He won't last—

MAN 6: Start sweatin blood, coon!

(FRED, *sweating and frantic, comes through side door*)

FRED: I warned you, I warned you—

POP: Get back inside—

FRED: Can'tya—

SMITTY: Ssh!

POP: They won't cross us—

FRED: They nothing, it's HIM—

MAN 1: E-leven! (*"Ooh" from* CROWD *as* FRED *rushes back in*)

MAN 1: Right off, a low one—

MAN 7: You would, ya—

MAN 5: He can't help it, the Kid's belly's five feet off the—

(ROAR)

MAN 1: Missed him, nigger—

(*Enter the* AGENT—*heads for* POP *and* SMITTY)

(ROAR)

MAN 1: He slipped, the nigger slipped—

(ROAR)

Hit him, hit him again—Oh, you—

MAN 3: What—

(POP *and* AGENT *whisper*)

MAN 1: Don't just look at him!

MAN 7: No instink! No instink!

(AGENT *whispers to* SMITTY; SMITTY *runs inside*)

MAN 4: Let's get mad, Kid—

MAN 7: **A hundred and two degrees—Chalkasians ain't made for it—**

MAN 1: Oh, them clinches—

MAN 3: He holdin—?

MAN 1: Come—on—

(ROAR)

No, it's the nigger—! He's leanin, yeah—

MAN 4: **He's wearin down!**

MAN 3: **I toleya—**

MAN 1: Break it, ref—

MAN 2: Don't let him rest—

MAN 1: Oh, good man—

MAN 3: He wobblin—?

MAN 1: Sorta—yeah! Yeah! He's backin away there, he's wipin his eyes—

MAN 6: Go in on him—

MAN 1: He's goin—the nigger ain't—there, he's tryna dodge him—

(ROAR)

MAN 9: Run, tar-baby, run back to your barrel—

MAN 1: Boyoboy, yeah, **he's slowin down, he's—**

MAN 2: Let's go—

MAN 1: Shit—move in—

(SMITTY *re-enters with* RUDY, *the baseball player*)

AGENT: OK, Rudy—

RUDY: Who you, man—

MAN 6: MOVE IN!

AGENT: Get your shirt off—(*To* SMITTY) get him something to carry—

(SMITTY *dashes back inside*)

RUDY: Mah whut?

AGENT: (*tugging at the buttons*) That! Off! Like you put one on for him, remember—

MAN 1: No, Kid, chase him, he's tryna get his wind back—

RUDY: Whut de hell you—

AGENT: Get into that corner, Rudy, tell that pal of yours—

(ROAR—*drowns what he says*)

MAN 1: Be care—no, jab him off ya—Christ, the nigger's all over him, pile-drivin, whalin at him—cover up, he's—duck—Oh, Jesus, the Kid just—

RUDY: (*as* SMITTY *returns with towel and bottle*) Gimme dat, you mother—(*Seizes towel and bottle, and runs inside, pulling off his shirt*)

MAN 1: Cover, Kid, turn, turn—cover, he'll cave your ribs in—

(ROAR)

MAN 2: Stop the goddamn—

MAN 1: Wait, no, he's up—Oh the nigger's right in him, he's after it, he's—

MAN 6: Kid, don't let him—

MAN 1: All he's got, he's workin like a butcher—

MAN 2: No—

MAN 7: He's gotta—

MAN 5: Kid—Kid!—

MAN 9: Kid—

MAN 1: Hookin him, sluggin—oh, that eye—

MAN 6: Ride him out—

(NEGRO BOY *climbs up the other column to see*)

MAN 7: Kid—

MAN 6: Bust your hand, you—

MAN 1: Murder, it's murder—

MAN 4: No more—

MAN 2: Clinch him—

MAN 1: Ref—

MAN 6: Clinch him, dummox—

MAN 2: No more—

MAN 1: REF!

MAN 5: Stop it—

MAN 2: REF, YA—

NEGRO BOY: Eh! Eh! Eh! Eh!

MAN 1: He's on the ropes, he can't see, he's rollin, he's punchy—

MAN 2: How the hell does he—

(ROAR)

MAN 6: Is he—

MAN 1: No, it's a bell, lemme down . . . lemme down . . .
(*Slips down the column:* MAN 4 *is helped up to take his place*)

POP: (*to* SMITTY) Tell Fred to throw in the—

AGENT: (*to* SMITTY) Stay right here!

MAN 4: (*looking ring-ward*) God Almighty!

MAN 1: (*to* MAN 4) They workin on the eye?

MAN 4: Yeah, but the rest of him—! **Blood, welts all over**—

MAN 5: Fifty on the coon the next—

MAN 2: Shut your hole—

MAN 6: Don't worry, Kid—

MAN 1: **That eye came up like a grape!**

POP: (*to* AGENT) Oh, Mister—

PINKERTON MAN 1: (*offstage*) Comin through—(*Movement behind barrier*)

MAN 2: Jesus, the heat got him—

(PINKERTON MEN 1 *and* 2 *come through the gate carrying* GOLDIE *on a chair; the* AGENT *beckons to them*)

MAN 6: How you gonna fight without your Jew, spook—

GOLDIE: (*to* AGENT) Mister, it's no use, it's—

AGENT: Ssh!

MAN 4: Here they go—

(PINKERTON MEN *set* GOLDIE *down at the side door and run back inside*)

AGENT: (*to* GOLDIE) The boy get to him?

(ROAR)

MAN 4: Nigger's slouchin in there—

GOLDIE: Mister, he don't hear, he—

MAN 4: Little stiff on his pins there—the Kid's just waiting for it—

GOLDIE: **Like it's my son, I begged him!**

MAN 4: The nigger's feelin him out—the Kid's sorta rockin there—back up, Kid—please—

(ROAR)

The nigger roundhoused him—!

MAN 5: Here it comes—

(ROAR)

The Kid's still up—he's still up—tryna shake his head clear—the nigger don't know where to—

(ROAR *changes*)

MAN 2: Stay on your feet—

MAN 7: Kid—

MAN 4: He is! He is! The nigger can't do it—**he's hittin but he's outa juice! He's punched out!**

MAN 2: I knew it—

MAN 4: There! Nothin! Just stingin him, slappin him—

MAN 1: Kid—

MAN 6: He can't hurtya—

MAN 1: He's arm-heavy—

MAN 9: Please, Kid—

MAN 4: Look at him—He's saggin there, just heavin at you—

MAN 6: What the hell's he—

(ROAR)

MAN 4: He's hitting back! He's lashin at him—swingin there wild—

MAN 1: **He can't see—**

MAN 2: Kid—

MAN 4: **The coon's givin ground—**

MAN 7: Keep on swingin—

MAN 4: There, the coon's lurchin round him, he's—

MAN 6: Smell him out, Kid—

MAN 4: There—Oh—swiped him half across the ring—

MAN 1: (*pulling down* NEGRO BOY) Lemme up, you goddamn—

MAN 2: More—

MAN 3: It's gonna happen, Kid—

MAN 4: In on him, no, he's over—yeah—

MAN 7: Keep swinging—

MAN 4: Walkin in his sleep but he's after him—

MAN 6: Press him—

MAN 4: Just flailin them great big—

(ROAR)

Bango!

MAN 2: More, Kid!

MAN 7: Wheee!

MAN 1: (*on column*) Christ, it's like a noctopus!

MAN 2: Don't stop, Kid—

MAN 4: Ya shot it all, coon, can't hurt him!

MAN 9: Wahoo!

MAN 6: **Can't hurt nobody!**

(GOLDIE *totters to his feet and goes back inside*)

MAN 1: Kid, aim it lower—

MAN 4: Don't have to, he's reelin—

MAN 2: Lower—

MAN 7: He'll go under you—

MAN 4: No—got no legs left—

MAN 1: Bango!

MAN 2: Yippeee!

MAN 6: Give us the smile, coon—

MAN 1: He's flounderin—

MAN 2: Poleax him—

MAN 4: There—

MAN 1: Clap for that one, you—

MAN 4: Now, Kid—

MAN 2: Finish him—

MAN 1: The nigger can't hardly get his guard up—

MAN 2: Finish him—

MAN 4: It's comin—the Kid got him bulled into a corner—
punchin blind—

MAN 1: The blood's in both eyes—

MAN 2: (*and* OTHERS) Now—now—now—

MAN 4: Just goin like a windmill—

MAN 7: Oh, flatten him—

MAN 2: Wipe the rotten—

MAN 4: There—the nigger's grabbin for the rope—**he's bucklin**
—he's swingin with his other—

MAN 6: You're THROUGH—

MAN 4: The Kid's poundin right down on him, he's grabbin, he's hangin, he's holdin, he can't, the Kid's drivin him down like a big black—

(*Great* ROAR: MAN 1 *follows the referee's count with his own arm; his voice barely audible*)

MAN 1: Four—five—six—seven—eight—

(*The* CROWD'S ROAR *pulsates with the last two counts and pandemonium breaks loose: hugging, dancing, etc.*)

MAN 1: (*falling into arms below*) I love him, I love him—

(AGENT *leaves*)

MAN 2: Wahooo—

(POP *goes inside with* SMITTY)

MAN 6: **We got it—**

MAN 2: Yoweee—

MAN 6: Where's my fifty—

MAN 5: Let's get in there—

(THEY *all push at the barrier*)

MAN 2: What a Kid—

MAN 1: Quit the pushing—

(*Snatches of band music from within*)

MAN 4: They're bringin the nigger out—

184   THE GREAT WHITE HOPE

MAN 2: Who cares—

MAN 6: Open up—

MAN 7: We're missin all the—

MAN 6: Break it in, for—

MAN 2: (*as* THEY *break through*) WA-A-H-O-O-OH! (THEY ALL *rush in except* MAN 9, *who stops to throw a coin to* NEGRO BOY 2)

MAN 9: Here, chico—buy yourself a whitewash! (HE *follows the rest and the* BOY *runs off. The sounds of jubilation within rise still higher: the remaining* NEGRO BOY *climbs the column to watch*)

PINKERTON MAN 2: (*offstage*) Outa the way, come on, let 'em through here—

(JACK, *helped along by* TICK *and* GOLDIE *and escorted by four* PINKERTON MEN, *comes limping through the gates, the* PRESS *at his heels*)

PRESSMAN 1: Just a word, Jack—

PINKERTON MAN 2: Let's go boys—

GOLDIE: Not now—

PRESSMAN 2: Jack, in the tenth when you were—(*The music and crowd noise suddenly dwindle, and the faint but triumphant sound of the* ANNOUNCER'S VOICE *is heard.* JACK *stops*)

TICK: Les go, baby.

(JACK *stands listening*)

PRESSMAN 3: Jack—why do you think it happened? (JACK *stands listening*) I'm asking—(*The* VOICE *rises to its conclusion: great cheering: the* BOY *climbs down.* JACK *turns to* PRESSMAN 3) Why did it, Jack?

JACK: He beat me, dassall. Ah juss din have it. (*The* BOY *spits on him and darts away*) Ain't dat right, boy?

TICK: (*moving him on*) Take it slow, nice an slow . . .

PRESSMAN 3: But why, Jack? Really.

JACK: (*laughs, stops*) Oh, man. Ah ain't got dem reallies from de Year One . . . **An if any a you got em, step right down an say em.** (*Looks around at audience:* DRUM-BEATING *begins*) **No . . . you new here like Ah is**—(MUSIC: *A March Triumphal*) Come on Chillun! Let 'em pass by!

(*Spreading his arms,* HE *sweeps* TICK, GOLDIE, *and* 1 *or* 2 PRESSMEN *off to one side, moving slowly, as the cheering* CROWD *surges out through the gates. The* KID *rides on their shoulders: immobile in his white robe, with one gloved hand extended, the golden belt draped around his neck and a towel over his head—his smashed and reddened face is barely visible—*HE *resembles the lifelike wooden saints in Catholic processions. Joyfully his bearers parade him before the audience, and with a final cheer fling their straw hats into the air*)

CURTAIN

ABOUT THE AUTHOR

HOWARD SACKLER has had plays produced in the United States, Europe, and South America. Winner of the 1954 Maxwell Anderson Award and Chicago's Sergel Award, he has received grants from the Rockefeller and Littauer Foundations. A new play, *The Pastime of Monsieur Robert,* is scheduled for production by the American Conservatory Theatre under the direction of William Ball. Mr. Sackler is also well experienced as a director, with credits for nearly 200 recordings for Caedmon Records, as well as theater productions and the 1964 NBC television special, *Shakespeare, Soul of an Age.*